Teaching Films

In America, Whale Rider, Bend It Like Beckham

Worksheets with Instructions & Answer Keys

Erarbeitet von
Nancy Grimm

Vandenhoeck & Ruprecht

Aus der Reihe *eXplorations*

Herausgegeben von Laurenz Volkmann

Mit einer Zeichnung von Nadja Gropp (S. 37)

Bildquellen: S. 9 und S. 18: Nancy Grimm. S. 27, S. 34f. und S. 39f.: abgedruckt mit freundlicher Genehmigung von Pandora Film. S. 44, S. 48ff., S. 52 und S. 58f.: abgedruckt mit freundlicher Genehmigung von Paramount Home Entertainment / Highlight Communications GmbH.

Textquellen: S. 54: stark gekürzte und adaptierte Version der Filmkritik von Philip French, *The Observer*, 14. April 2002; Internetquelle: http://film.guardian.co.uk/News_Story/Critic_Review /Observer_review/0,,683987,00.html.

Bibliografische Information der Deutschen Nationalbibliothek

Die Deutsche Nationalbibliothek verzeichnet diese Publikation in der Deutschen Nationalbibliografie; detaillierte bibliografische Daten sind im Internet über http://dnb.d-nb.de abrufbar.

ISBN: 978-3-525-79006-9

Printed in Germany
Druck und Bindung: ⊕ Hubert & Co. Göttingen

Gedruckt auf alterungsbeständigem Papier

Inhalt

Einführung

Filme im Englischunterricht

Filme spielen im gesamten Prozess des Lehrens und Lernens von Fremdsprachen eine wichtige Rolle. In dieser Funktion wurden und werden sie auch im Englischunterricht genutzt und eingesetzt. Die Analyse der Ist-Situation bezüglich des Einsatzes von Filmen zeigt, dass deren Potenzial – gerade auch in Hinsicht auf die sich in den letzten Jahren rasant entwickelnde DVD-Technik – stellenweise noch nicht vollständig genutzt wird.

Ein wesentlicher Vorteil bei der Beschäftigung mit Filmen im Unterricht liegt in der Tatsache, dass dieses Medium seitens der Lernenden im Alltag sehr häufig aufgenommen wird. Diese Rezeption ist oft eher passiver, interessengebundener Art. Dennoch kann man Schülerinnen und Schüler verschiedenster Altersstufen genau an diesem Punkt abholen, z.B. mit Filmen, die ihrer Lebenswirklichkeit entsprechen und zu einer aktiven Auseinandersetzung mit ihnen oft nahe stehenden Themen motivieren.

Dennoch sollte der Prozess der Auswahl von Filmen nicht ausschließlich am Interesse der Lernenden orientiert sein. Gerade im Hinblick auf die Entwicklung und Förderung interkultureller Kompetenz, einschließlich der Fähigkeiten zum Perspektivenwechsel, zur Perspektivenübernahme und zur Perspektivenkoordinierung, bietet sich eine breite Auswahl von Filmen an. Diese stehen aufgrund ihrer Thematik, künstlerischen Umsetzung und kulturellen Verortung nicht von vornherein im Fokus der jugendlichen Interessenlage. Hier eröffnen sich aber im Erkunden von bestimmten Brüchen im Vergleich zur eigenen Lebensweise oder zu den eigenen Erwartungshaltungen vielfältige Sprechanlässe.

Diese kommunikativen Unterrichtssituationen befördern die Entwicklung von Kompetenzen in den Bereichen Hören, Sehen und Verstehen und unterstützen die in Lehr- und Rahmenplänen vieler Länder fixierte Umsetzung von Sprachfunktionen wie Erzählen, Beschreiben und Argumentieren. Eine vertiefende Filmanalyse trägt nicht zuletzt zur Entwicklung von komplexen Diskursqualitäten wie dem Diskutieren, Vermitteln, Meinungen aushandeln und vertreten sowie dem Argumentieren bei.

Filme stellen in ihrer Komplexität gleichzeitig auch eine enorme Herausforderung für Lernende und Lehrende dar. Hierbei kommt es darauf an, bereits im frühen Lernalter der Schülerinnen und Schüler Strategien zu entwickeln und zu üben, die auf diese Mehrdimensionalität ausgerichtet sind. Eines der in dieser Hinsicht produktiven Konzepte ist das der Intertextualität, welches in vielfältiger Weise in dem vorliegenden Material aufgegriffen wird. So können sich Filme aufeinander beziehen, Soundtracks sind z.B. nicht nur schmückendes Beiwerk, sondern vermitteln – teilweise kontrastiv – Inhalte und Werte. Nicht zuletzt können im Film durch eine einzige Kameraeinstellung mehrdimensionale Geschichten innerhalb kürzester Zeit erzählt werden. Die dafür notwendigen Erschließungstechniken müssen den Schülerinnen und Schülern bewusst gemacht werden.

Diese Techniken, welche nicht nur rein handwerklich zu verstehen sind, sondern auch eine inhaltliche und wertorientierende Funktion haben, bilden einen medienerzieherischen Schwerpunkt. Die Sprache von Filmen umfasst mehr als nur Bilder, Texte und Soundtracks. Zur Bedeutung der Herausbildung von Medienkompetenz durch Filme heißt es im Vorwort zu Susan Stempleskis und Barry Tomalins hilfreicher Handreichung *Film* (2001) wie folgt:

> We live in a culture dominated by the visual image, and in particular, the moving image. The written word has, to a large extent, ceded its pre-eminence to visual representations of the world which in turn has created the need for us to make sense of this visual rhetoric. *Moving pictures have a grammar and discourse all their own which we need to decode if we are to understand the meanings that they contain.* (Maley in Stempleski & Tomalin 2001, meine Hervorhebung)

Das heißt, je mehr man vom „Gesamtkunstwerk“ erfasst, selbst erkundet und in Beziehung zur eigenen Lebenswirklichkeit zu setzen vermag, desto höher ist zum einen der intellektuelle Gewinn. Zum anderen entwickelt sich die Fähigkeit zur kritischen, reflektierenden Rezeption und damit wachsen die Freude und das Interesse an qualitativ hochwertigen Filmbeiträgen.

Zu den ausgewählten Filmen

Das vorliegende Material soll aufgrund seiner Informationsdichte und mittels der integrierten Arbeitsblätter zum einen die Unterrichtsvorbereitungen erleichtern und gleichzeitig motivierend sowohl für Lernende als auch Lehrende sein. Die bewusst vorgenommene Mischung bekannter und weniger bekannter Filme (Machart, Besetzung, kulturelles Umfeld) spiegelt auch die Vielfalt der intendierten Schüleraktivitäten unter Verwendung verschiedenster Sozialformen wider.

Die vorgestellten Aktivitäten treffen eine Auswahl aus zahlreichen Vorschlägen, die es für die Arbeit mit Filmen gibt. Sie können nahezu unendlich erweitert werden. Typische Vorschläge sind der Buch- und Filmvergleich, das so genannte „What if-Spiel“, welches anregt, über alternative Handlungsverläufe zu spekulieren, oder das darstellende Spielen. Stempleski und Tomalin bieten in ihrer Handreichung *Film* zahlreiche hilfreiche Ideen für die Arbeit mit Filmen. Einige sollen hier als erweiterter Ideenpool überblicksartig dargestellt werden:

- Umfrage: Lieblingsfilme, Lieblingssoundtrack, Lieblingsschauspieler/innen
- Analyse und Vergleich von Filmtrailern
- Erstellen eines Filmskripts aus einem Romanausschnitt
- Vergleich von englischer Originalversion und deutscher Synchronisation (Titel, Dialoge, Untertitel, etc.)
- Interviews mit Filmcharakteren
- Projekt: Filmmagazin
- Projekt: Erstellen eines eigenen Kurzfilms, Trailers, Soundtracks

Daneben sei an dieser Stelle vor allem auch auf das Extramaterial (Audiokommentar, ausgelassene Szenen, Fotogalerien, Interviews, etc.) verwiesen, das mittlerweile auf vielen DVDs enthalten ist. Dieses kann vielfach in die Auseinandersetzung mit Filmen einbezogen werden.

Die hier vorgestellten Unterrichtsvorschläge können als Paradigma für die Behandlung anderer Filme und damit verbundener Themen und Ziele genutzt werden. Das vorliegende Material hat es sich zur Aufgabe gemacht, Anregungen für einen möglichst handlungsorientierten, offenen Unterricht zu geben und gleichzeitig medienkritische Impulse zu setzen. Die Auswahl der Filme und ihre Behandlung soll in ihrer Bandbreite möglichst viele Erfordernisse der Lehr- und Rahmenpläne der Länder abdecken.

Einführung

Der Film *In America* (2002) spiegelt die irische Einwandererperspektive in der Auseinandersetzung mit der amerikanischen Kultur. Mit dem neuseeländischen Film *Whale Rider* (2003) begibt sich der Zuschauer auf eine Reise in die Kultur und Vorstellungswelt der Maori. Gleichzeitig erzählt der Film die Geschichte eines Generationskonflikts und bietet so Identifikationspotenzial für die Lernenden. In Verbindung dazu handelt es sich bei dem mittlerweile sehr bekannten *Bend It Like Beckham* (2002) um einen Film, der vor allem aufgrund seiner Thematik des Aushandelns von Toleranz in der Begegnung von Kulturen im Hinblick auf interkulturelles Lernen wichtig ist. Hierzu betont Laurenz Volkmann:

> Interkulturelle Kompetenz im *global village,* in der Welt der sich ständig durch neue Technologien und Modernisierungsschübe einander annähernden Kulturen, bedeutet nicht allein die Notwendigkeit, verschiedene Kommunikationsstrategien einzuüben. [...] Vielmehr geht es auch darum, andere Wertvorstellungen zu akzeptieren und von ihnen zu lernen. Es geht dabei auch um eine andere Ethik des Umgangs mit dem Fremden, die den Herausforderungen der zunehmend interdependenter werdenden Weltgesellschaft adäquat ist. (Volkmann in: *Wie Ist Fremdverstehen Lehr- und Lernbar,* 2000: 177)

Alle Filme sind problemlos auch in Deutschland zu kaufen oder auszuleihen, beispielsweise online über www.amazon.de: *In America* (DVD, ASIN: B000149MCQ), *Whale Rider* (DVD, ASIN: B0001BUK1C), *Bend It Like Beckham* (DVD, ASIN: B00007JQTG).

Aufbau des Materials

Das vorliegende Material stellt zu jedem der ausgewählten Filme eine Unterrichtsreihe vor, die den Film in seiner Ganzheit als eigenständiges Unterrichtsthema betrachtet und dennoch zeitlich übersichtlich gestaltet ist. Jede Unterrichtsreihe ist inklusive der Zeit für das Ansehen des Films auf ca. vier bis fünf Doppelstunden (ca. 8 bis 10 Einzelstunden) angelegt. Jedem Film ist ein informativer und anleitender Teil für die Unterrichtenden vorangestellt. In diesem sind neben Hintergrundinformationen zu den einzelnen Filmen vor allem auch konkrete Anleitungen zur Durchführung der Unterrichtsreihe enthalten. Die Struktur der Anleitungen folgt der Einteilung jeder Unterrichtsreihe in *pre-*, *while-* und *post-viewing*-Aktivitäten. Diese sind auf kopierbaren Arbeitsblättern grafisch übersichtlich dargestellt und mit Anleitungen in den Lehrerinformationen (*teacher's section*) versehen. Eine Auswahl möglicher Antworten ist anschließend im Lösungsschlüssel (*answer key*) hinterlegt.

Erklärung der Symbole

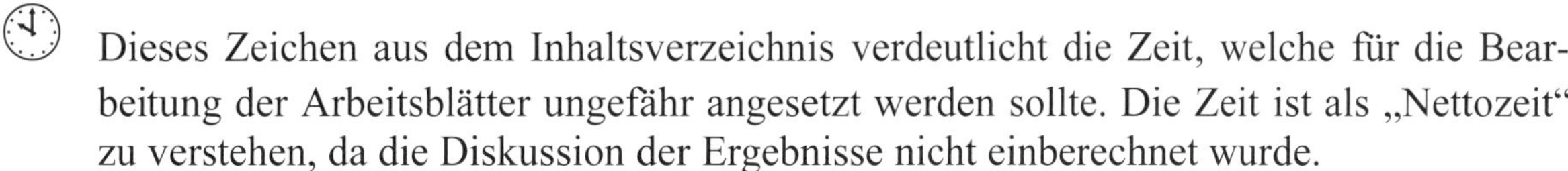

Dieses Zeichen aus dem Inhaltsverzeichnis verdeutlicht die Zeit, welche für die Bearbeitung der Arbeitsblätter ungefähr angesetzt werden sollte. Die Zeit ist als „Nettozeit" zu verstehen, da die Diskussion der Ergebnisse nicht einberechnet wurde.

Neben diesem Symbol kann die Bearbeitungszeit, welche das Inhaltsverzeichnis als flexibel adaptierbaren Zeitrahmen vorgibt, auf den Arbeitsblättern vermerkt werden.

Auf Seiten mit diesem Symbol bietet das Material eine kurze Zusammenfassung des Films sowie mit dem Film verbundenes Material.

Dieses Symbol indiziert Arbeitsblätter mit Aufgaben, welche konkret mit der Analyse bestimmter Filmszenen bzw. des gesamten Films verbunden sind.

 Mit diesem Symbol sind Arbeitsblätter versehen, die Aufgaben enthalten, welche zur Diskussion anregen und Gesprächsanlässe bieten.

 Dieses Symbol kennzeichnet Arbeitsblätter mir Höraufgaben.

 Diese Arbeitsblätter enthalten Aufgaben zu Filmcharakteren.

 Auf Arbeitsblättern mit diesem Symbol werden Aufgaben zur Auseinandersetzung mit Filmsprache gestellt.

 Dieses Symbol kennzeichnet Arbeitsblätter, auf denen Lernende zur Produktion von Texten angeregt werden.

 Arbeitsblätter mit diesem Symbol enthalten Aufgaben, die eine WebQuest oder die Arbeit mit dem Computer/Internet beinhalten.

Ausgewählte Buch- und Internetquellen zum Thema

Die hier ausgewählten Titel setzen sich konkret mit der Filmanalyse und dem Einsatz von Filmen im Englischunterricht auseinander. Des Weiteren sind Werke ausgesucht, die sich mit dem Thema „Interkulturelle Kompetenz" beschäftigen. Diese Materie wie auch die Möglichkeit der Vermittlung interkultureller Kompetenz ist allen Filmen ein zentrales Anliegen.

Gast, Wolfgang: *Film und Literatur: Analysen, Materialien, Unterrichtsvorschläge. Einführung in Begriffe und Methoden der Filmanalyse.* Frankfurt/Main: Diesterweg, 1993

Hildebrand, Jens: *Film: Ratgeber für Lehrer*. Köln: Aulis, 2001

Phillips, William H.: *Film: An Introduction*. 3. Aufl. Palgrave MacMillan, 2005

Stempleski, Susan & Tomalin, Barry: *Film*. Oxford: OUP, 2001

---. *Video in Action: Recipes for Using Video in Language Teaching*. New York & London: Prentice Hall, 1990

Steinmetz, Rüdiger: *Filme sehen lernen: Grundlagen der Filmästhetik*. Frankfurt/Main: Zweitausendeins, 2003 (nur vom Verlag erhältlich, www.Zweitausendeins.de)

Tomalin, Barry & Stempleski, Susan: *Cultural Awareness*. Oxford: OUP, 1993

Volkmann, Laurenz; Stierstorfer, Klaus & Gehring, Wolfgang: *Interkulturelle Kompetenz*. Tübingen: Narr, 2002

Filminformationen: http://www.imdb.com, http://allmovie.com, http://www.filmsite.org
Filmkritiken: http://www.rottentomatoes.com, http://filmcritic.com
British Film Institute: http://www.bfi.org.uk
Filmskripte: http://www.geocities.com/hollywood/9371/scriptlist1.htm
Screenplays: http://dir.yahoo.com/Entertainment/Movies_and_Film/Screenplays
Filmportal: http://dir.yahoo.com/Entertainment/Movies_and_Film
Medienarbeit: http://www.kinofenster.de, http://www.mediamanual.at

In den Anleitungen zu den einzelnen Unterrichtsreihen wird an entsprechender Stelle auf weitere ergänzende Literatur oder auf Internetseiten verwiesen.

Viel Erfolg und Spaß!

In America: Teacher's section

Zum Film

In America eignet sich in vielerlei Hinsicht in ganz besonderem Maße für den Einsatz im Unterricht.

Zunächst zeigt der Film den Kampf und das Leben einer irischen Familie auf, welche mit einer neuen, kleineren Einwanderungswelle in den 1980ziger Jahren illegal in die USA immigrierte. Hinsichtlich der Umsetzung aktueller Konzepte der *cultural studies* im Unterricht bietet sich mit diesem Film also eine Diskussion über die Immigrationsproblematik an. Zudem ergibt sich durch die irische Nationalität der Einwandererfamilie in diesem Film die Möglichkeit, einen Diskurs über die Genese der besonders ausgeprägten Stereotypisierung der irischen Bevölkerungsgruppe zu führen. Hierbei erweisen sich folgende Internetquellen als hilfreich:

- http://allaboutirish.com/library/identity/stereotypes.shtm
- www.nde.state.ne.us/SS/irish/unit_2.html

American flag, photographed in Manhattan, New York, 2002

Des Weiteren ist der Film ein filmisches Meisterwerk des irischen Regisseurs Jim Sheridan, der hier die eigene autobiografische Erfahrung der Immigration in die USA, aber auch den Verlust seines Bruders Frankie thematisiert: „All the events are true except that it was my brother who died so I made myself my father and my wife my mother – I don't know what that means – and my daughter myself." Sheridan gab sein Filmdebüt mit *My Left Foot* (1989), der zwei Oscar-Nominierungen erhielt. Es folgten weitere erfolgreiche Filme wie *The Field* (1990), *In the Name of the Father* (1993) und *The Boxer* (1997).

Das Skript für *In America* wurde von Sheridan und seinen beiden Töchtern verfasst. So entstand ein Manuskript, welches das Leben in New York aus drei verschiedenen Perspektiven beleuchtet. Dieser Umstand spiegelt sich auch in der filmerzählerischen Umsetzung. Die Subjektivität und Perspektivenvielfalt des Films wird vor allem durch die stellenweise subjektive Kameraführung realisiert. Hierbei ist die Verwendung eines Camcorders und zahlreicher *voice-over*, um eine mithin kindliche Subjektivität zu erzeugen, besonders prägnant. Empfohlen sei zudem das Buch *In America: A Portrait of the Film* (Newmarket Press, 2003) von Jim, Naomi und Kirsten Sheridan.

Der Film arbeitet mit den Konventionen des Magischen Realismus. Fantasie-, märchen- und geisterhafte Motive fließen hierbei in die reale Welt der Filmcharaktere ein. Die drei Wünsche, über die Christy verfügt, um ihrer Familie zu helfen, werden als wohlbekanntes Märchenmotiv übernommen. Das Märchen *Jack and the Beanstalk* wird sogar direkt im Film zitiert. Daneben unterstützt die Figur des an HIV erkrankten Künstlers Mateo die mystischen Elemente im Film. Die filmische Umsetzung dieser magischen Elemente stellt eine besondere

Leistung des Films dar und sollte durch eine Auswahl passender Szenen und Sequenzen ganz bewusst in seine Besprechung aufgenommen werden.

In America wird voraussichtlich höchst emotional rezipiert. Dabei ist es vor allem die überzeugende und überaus natürliche darstellerische Leistung der Filmdebütantinnen Sarah und Emma Bolger in den Rollen der Kinder Ariel und Christy, die dem Film seinen besonderen Charme verleiht. Samantha Morton, die neben Paddy Considine (Johnny) den Part der Mutter Sarah spielt, nominierte man aufgrund ihrer überzeugenden Darstellung für einen Oscar (Beste Hauptdarstellerin).

Zur Durchführung der Unterrichtsreihe

Der recht lange (101 Minuten, ab 12 Jahren) und für die Sekundarstufe II geeignete Film sollte in zwei Sequenzen in zwei Doppelstunden mit anschließender Diskussion der Fragen zum Film gezeigt werden. Von einer weiteren Sequenzialisierung sollte aufgrund des emotionalen Gehalts des Films und seiner erzählerischer Wirkung abgesehen werden. Flexibel adaptierbare Zeitrahmen für die Bearbeitung der Arbeitsblätter sind dem Inhaltsverzeichnis zu entnehmen.

Die einführenden *viewing*-Sequenzen werden von konkreten Fragen begleitet (WS 1a/1b). Die Arbeit mit diesen Fragen kann auf unterschiedliche Weise erfolgen und sollte auf die Klassensituation abgestimmt sein. Zum einen bietet es sich an, jeweils eine Frage durch eine Gruppe von Lernenden beantworten und anschließend diskutieren zu lassen. Zum anderen können die Fragen auch in ihrer Gesamtheit durch alle Lernenden gelöst werden und dann in einer Klassendiskussion besprochen werden. Eine Filmzusammenfassung greift danach den Inhalt des Films nochmals auf und bietet eine Grundlage für die weitere Besprechung des Films (WS 2).

Die Arbeit mit dem Film setzt sich fort mit einer vertieften Beschäftigung mit jeweils einem (1) intertextuellen, einem (2) sozialhistorischen, einem (3) filmtechnischen und einem (4) intertextuell-medialen Schwerpunkt innerhalb von „Expertengruppen". Die offene und darüber hinaus handlungsorientierte Unterrichtsform der Expertengruppe fördert nicht nur soziale Kompetenzen, sondern unterstützt das selbstverantwortliche Lernen in einem Team. Zudem müssen sich die Schüler Gedanken über die Form der Präsentation ihrer Ergebnisse machen. Die Eckpunkte, die für eine erfolgreiche Präsentation erforderlich sind, könnten zuvor mit Hilfe eines Tafelbildes diskutiert bzw. wiederholt werden:

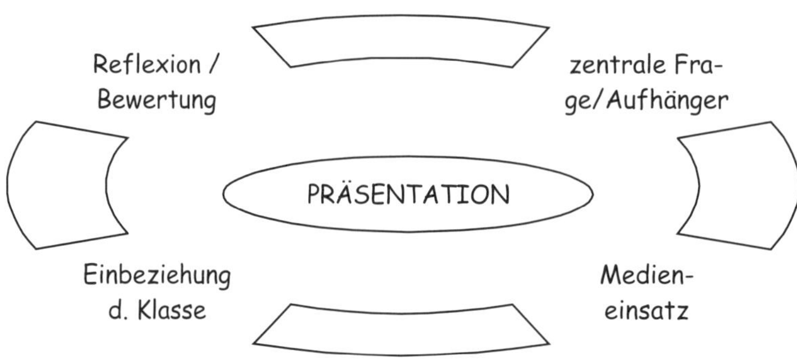

Die erste Expertengruppe (WS 3a-3c) konzentriert sich auf den intertextuellen Verweis auf das Märchen *Jack and the Beanstalk*, das auf den Arbeitsblättern für die Lernenden wiedergegeben ist. Neben einer Vorstellung der Geschichte und deren „Moral" bzw. Hauptaussage sollte sich diese Expertengruppe vor allem mit der Verbindung zwischen dem Märchen und einer zentralen Filmszene auseinandersetzen. Dabei sollte die Bedeutung der Verwendung märchenhafter Elemente für den Film herausgestellt werden.

Eine zweite Expertengruppe (WS 4a/4b) soll entstehungsgeschichtliche Hintergrundinformationen zum Thema „Halloween" zusammentragen. Dabei kann auf eigene Erfahrungen mit diesem Feiertag zurückgegriffen werden, da diese Tradition auch in Deutschland zunehmend gepflegt wird, ohne dass konkretes Wissen über ihre Entstehungsgeschichte existiert. In einem weiteren Schritt werden die Hintergrundinformationen auf eine Filmszene angewendet, die nicht nur eine amerikanische Halloween-Feier zeigt, sondern auch das Thema der Assimilation in den Mittelpunkt stellt. Die Lernenden diskutieren, wie sich die Familie auf unterschiedliche Weise dieser Problematik stellt.

Die dritte Expertengruppe (WS 5a/5b) geht auf die filmerzählerische Subjektivität des Films ein. In einem Filmzitat wird der Umstand angesprochen, dass Christy alle ihre Erfahrungen ihrem Camcorder wie einem Tagebuch erzählt und gleichermaßen Ereignisse mit ihrem Camcorder festhält. Diese Art der Erzählung soll von den Lernenden anhand einer zentralen Filmszene nachvollzogen und beschrieben werden. In einem weiteren Schritt diskutieren die Experten die Veränderung der subjektiven Erzählung, wenn diese plötzlich durch Ariel, die jüngere Schwester, artikuliert wird. Die Lernenden schreiben die Filmszene dann aus der Sicht Ariels als *voice-over* um.

Eine vierte Expertengruppe (WS 6a/6b) nimmt intermedial auf den Soundtrack des Films Bezug. Hierbei steht das Lied „Desperado" (The Eagles) im Vordergrund, welches eine Filmszene unterlegt. Die Experten rekonstruieren den Liedtext und diskutieren dessen Inhalt. Diese Diskussion wird durch einen Fokus auf das Wort „desperado" vertieft. Es gilt zu hinterfragen, welche Nuancen des Wortes „desperado" auf Johnny anzuwenden bzw. zu verwerfen sind. Abschließend diskutieren die Experten, in welcher Form sich die Musik mit der Filmszene in Verbindung bringen lässt und wie sie diese atmosphärisch unterstützt.

Die Arbeit in den Expertengruppen ist für die Bearbeitung der Arbeitsblätter auf 45 Minuten angelegt. Die Präsentationen sollten mit entsprechendem Medieneinsatz und unter Beteiligung der Mitschüler den Zeitraum von 20 Minuten nicht überschreiten.

Im Anschluss an die Arbeit in Expertengruppen könnte der Schlussteil des Films einer näheren Betrachtung unterzogen werden (WS 7). Da es verstärkt die Elemente des Magischen Realismus nutzt, mag das Ende als ein typisches *happy ending* bezeichnet werden, was in Filmkritiken oft bemängelt wurde. Jim Sheridan verbindet mit diesem Schluss jedoch eine ganz besondere, Fragen der stereotypen Geschlechterkategorisierung aufwerfende Aussage, die auf der DVD im Kommentar des Regisseurs als Hör- und Vokabelaufgabe nachvollzogen und diskutiert werden kann.

Viewing

Task 1: While watching the first part of the movie (0:00:00 - 0:56:05), take notes to answer the following questions.

(1) Why did the family decide to come to the USA?

____

____

____

(2) How would you describe the first impression they get of New York?

____

____

____

(3) What kind of housing does the family eventually reside in? How does Ariel refer to it?

____

____

____

(4) Which (leit)motif recurs at the fun fair-scene?

____

____

____

(5) Which character is introduced when Johnny is playing "Fee, fie, foe, fum..." with the children? Describe your first impression of this character.

____

____

____

(6) Johnny cannot "feel" the unborn baby. Why?

____

____

____

⌛____ minutes

In America: Worksheet 1b

Task 2: Before watching the second part of the movie (0:56:05 – 1:39:00), have a look at the dialogue below. What do you think may have happened?

Christy: "What's wrong?"
Ariel: "He never said goodbye."
Christy: "What?"
Ariel: "He never said goodbye."

Task 3: Continue watching the movie. Take more notes to answer the following questions.

(7) Sitting sick in his chair, what can be said about the disease Mateo is suffering from? What is special about the character of Ariel in this scene?

____

____

____

(8) Describe the symbolism inherent in cutting back and forth between the rapping stockbroker and the lifeless Mateo?

____

____

____

(9) What happens when Mateo dies?

____

____

____

⌛____ minutes

Movie synopsis

Task: Fill in the gaps with words from the vocabulary box.

Johnny and Sarah, a young Irish couple, and their two daughters, Christy and Ariel, (1) ________________ the USA illegally via the Canadian border. They are (2) ___________ for Manhattan, NYC, where they hope to find an apartment. They end up in a skimpy apartment in Hell's Kitchen, one of the worst parts of Manhattan. The parents struggles to (3) _________________ from the death of their son Frankie.

Johnny, an unemployed actor, is auditioning while earning a living for the family as a taxi driver. His wife, a former teacher, (4) _________________ house and (5) ______________ tables in a little ice cream parlor. While the financial problems of the family are severe, the two daughters initially experience their life in New York City as an enormous adventure. The two daughters even (6) _________________ to enter Mateo's apartment, although the writing on his door tells intruders to "[k]eep away". Mateo (7) ___________ the family and soon becomes their companion. When it turns out that Mateo is dying of HIV and has to be hospitalized, things are initially changing for the worse.

Sarah (8) ________________ birth to her daughter prematurely. The infant's condition is poor and doctor's are trying to (9) _______________ her life by giving her a blood transfusion. Christy's blood is the only one matching and she comes to give her blood for the new-born.

However, far from improving, the infant's health is declining and so are Mateo's health and the family's financial situation. Mateo (10) ____________ at the end of the movie, but the baby's health is improving. Besides, the family's hospital bill has been (11) _______ by Mateo. With an ending that is not only happy, but also highly symbolic and magical, the family's bond is (12) _____ ______________ as Ariel is greeted by E.T. Eventually, Johnny is enabled to say goodbye to his departed son, Frankie.

Vocabulary box

tends	enter	gives
headed	waits	recover
dies	paid	dare
save	befriends	strengthened

⌛____ minutes

Expert Group 1: Jack and the Beanstalk

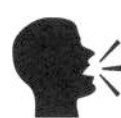

During the movie we witness a scene that alludes to the famous English folktale Jack and the Beanstalk. *Johnny is chasing his children, chanting the slightly adapted lines "Fee, fie, foe, fum. I smell the blood of an Irishman [...]!" from the tale.*

 Jack and the Beanstalk

The author of Jack and the Beanstalk, an old British folktale, was almost certainly British. The tale's origins, however, are quite uncertain. Evidence shows that the tale was part of the 1734-edition of Round About Our Coal Fire, an early collection of stories for children. There exist slightly different versions, but the story of Jack fighting a giant is always the same.

Task 1: Read through the tale of Jack and the Beanstalk on this and the next page.

Jack and the Beanstalk

"It's no good," said Jack's mother. "We shall have to sell our cow. We have no money left and you are such a lazy, silly boy, Jack, that you will never find work."

So Jack set off to market with the cow, but on the way he met a stranger. "Why walk all the way to market?" asked the man. "I will take the cow off your hands right away and I'll give you these magic beans in return. I think you'll agree, that's a bargain!"

Jack was delighted to have a handful of magic beans and he handed over the cow immediately. But Jack's mother was furious. "You are a stupid, idle boy!" she cried, "and you will go straight to bed without any supper!" And she threw the beans out of the window.

The next morning when Jack woke up, he thought that the room seemed very dark. He looked out of the window and was astonished to see that an enormous bean plant had grown beside the house. Its top disappeared into the clouds.

Now Jack was a lazy boy, but he was brave, too. He clambered out of the window and began to climb up the beanstalk.

Jack climbed and climbed until he came to the top of the beanstalk in a land above the clouds. Far away he could see a huge castle and he set off to walk towards it. Just as night was falling, he reached the great wooden door and knocked loudly.

A woman came to the door and looked at him in surprise. "You can't stay here," she said. "My husband, the ogre, eats little boys!"

But Jack explained that he was tired and hungry and at last the woman relented and let him come in for some bread and cheese. No sooner had Jack begun to eat when he felt the floor begin to shake.

"It's my husband!" cried the woman. "Hide in the oven, quick!" The ogre's mighty feet thundered across the floor and his huge voice bellowed across the room. “*Fee, fie, foe, fum, I smell the blood of an Englishman. Be he alive, or be he dead, I’ll grind his bones to make my bread.*”

“Nonsense,” said his wife. “That’s just the soup ready for your supper.” So the ogre sat down and ate his soup. When he had finished, he called to his wife, “Bring me my hen!” His wife went out and fetched a white hen.

The ogre took the hen and shouted, “Lay!” To Jack’s amazement as he peeped out of the oven door, the hen laid a golden egg! Again and again the ogre ordered the hen to lay, until there were twelve golden eggs on the table. Then the ogre fell asleep and began to snore.

When he heard the ogre snoring, Jack jumped out of the oven, picked up the magic hen, and ran away as fast as his legs would carry him. He scrambled down the beanstalk and stood, breathless, in front of his mother.

“Why Jack!” she cried. “That is the hen that the wicked ogre stole from your father. Now our troubles are over!”

But although Jack and his mother became quite wealthy, the boy still had a spirit of adventure. One day he climbed the beanstalk again and made his way to the ogre’s castle. Once again he hid and heard the ogre’s voice. “*Fee, fie, foe, fum, I smell the blood of an Englishman. Be he alive, or be he dead, I’ll grind his bones to make my bread.*”

The ogre’s wife brought him his supper and Jack was safe. After supper, the ogre called for his money bags. As Jack watched, he counted out bags and bags of gold coins.

“As soon as he falls asleep, I will take those money bags,” said Jack to himself. And so he did. Again, Jack’s mother was delighted. “This money belonged to your father, too,” she said.

Jack decided to climb the beanstalk one more time. Everything happened just as before but this time after supper the ogre called for his golden harp. When the ogre’s wife brought the harp to the table, the ogre commanded, “Play!” At once the harp began to play the sweetest music Jack had ever heard.

No sooner had the ogre fallen asleep than Jack seized the harp and ran out of the door. But the harp called out, “Master! Master!” and the ogre awoke. With thundering footsteps, he chased after the boy. Jack ran as fast as he could to the top of the beanstalk but all the time he could hear the ogre getting nearer and nearer. He scrambled down as quickly as he could, but the ogre followed him. When he was nearly at the bottom, Jack called out. “Mother, mother, bring the axe!” Jack took the axe and with one great blow he cut through the huge beanstalk. The ogre came tumbling down to his death.

As for Jack and his mother, they lived happily ever after.

Task 2: Summarize the story in a few sentences.

Summary: ______________________________

____

____

____

____

____

In America: Worksheet 3c

Task 3: Explain the central message of the tale.

Notes:____

____

____

____

____

____

____

Task 4: Discuss why director Jim Sheridan decided to include a reference to Jack and the Beanstalk in his movie. After re-watching the scene (0:25:40 - 0:27:00), describe its atmosphere and how it changes during the scene.

Notes:____

____

____

____

____

____

____

____

____

____

____

____

____

____

____

____

____

____

⌛____ minutes

Expert Group 2: Halloween

Pumpkins – the quintessential Halloween items

Task 1: Find out facts and figures about Halloween – an originally Celtic holiday – and how it is celebrated today. Use the website below:

- http://www.historychannel.com/exhibits/halloween

Ancient Origins: ______________________________

____

____

____

____

____

____

____

Modern Traditions: ______________________________

____

____

____

____

____

____

____

In America: Worksheet 4b

After the somewhat awkward Halloween party in Christy's and Ariel's school, the family goes home. On the way home, Christy tosses the prize for "Best Homemade Costume" into the trash can and the following dialogue unfolds (0:37:30 – 0:39:10):

Christy:	"They made it [the prize] up 'cause they pity us."
Johnny:	"You got it 'cause you're different."
Ariel:	"We don't want to be different. We want to be the same as everybody else."
Johnny:	"Why would you want to be the same as everybody else?"
Ariel:	"But everybody else goes trick-or-treating."
Sarah:	"What's that?"
Ariel:	"It's what they do here for Halloween."

Task 2: Analyze the differences between the parents and their daughters in adapting to their new life in America.

Parents	Daughters

ⓘ Assimilation

The process whereby a minority group gradually adopts the customs and attitudes of the dominant culture.

Task 3: Should immigrants assimilate to American (or German) culture? Discuss.

⌛____ minutes

Expert Group 3: Narrative perspective

After having watched E.T.*, a movie about a lonely extraterrestrial on earth, in the movie theater, the family goes into the ice cream parlor. In this scene (0:19:12 - 0:19:50), the following dialogue unfolds:*

Ariel:	"I miss things."
Johnny:	"What do you miss?"
Ariel:	"Things, I've no one to play with."
Johnny:	"You have your sister to play with."
Ariel:	"No, she plays with her camcorder. And I've no one to tell my secrets to. Christy tells them to her camcorder. And she won't let me hear what she says. And you don't play with us anymore."

This dialogue plays with the narrative perspective of the movie. Christy records what happens with her camcorder and comments on it in retrospect.

Task 1: After the above mentioned scene, the family goes to a fun fair, where Johnny tries to win an E.T.-doll for Ariel. Re-watch the scene (0:20:15 - 0:25:25) and summarize what Christy says in the voice-over for this scene. Describe what is typical of Christy's narration.

Notes:____

In America: Worksheet 5b

Task 2: Imagine that a shift in the narrative perspective occurs. Suddenly, Ariel is the narrator. Describe the consequences for the narration.

Notes:____

Task 3: Watch the scene once again and write a new voice-over that conveys Ariel's more childlike point of view.

Notes:____

⌛____ minutes

Expert Group 4: Music

In the movie songs are used as part of the action. This is specifically obvious in the case of the song "Desperado" by The Eagles sung by Christy while her father is filming her.

Task 1: Reconstruct ten phrases consisting of 3 up to 5 words from the words in the table below. Proceed from left to right and stick to the order of words as given in the table (see example 1).

(1) out ✓	to	your	senses	get
(2) laid	ones	of	pleasing	
(3) is	that	fences ✓	your	
(4) the	your	are	diamonds	
(5) things	riding ✓	you	bet	
(6) a	queen	your	can't	you
(7) come	have	above	table	
(8) let	rainbow	got	you	
(9) the	somebody	love		reasons
(10) you	upon	best	you	

1 out riding fences______________________________
2 ____
3 ____
4 ____
5 ____
6 ____
7 ____
8 ____
9 ____
10 ____

Task 2: Find the original version of the lyrics of "Desperado" by accessing www.seeklyrics.com and check if you have matched the right words.

Task 3: Use a dictionary to find a definition for the word "desperado" and write it down.

Desperado:____

____

____

Task 4: There are a number of synonyms for the word "desperado" such as "criminal", "outlaw", "gangster", "villain", or "crook". Are these words appropriate to describe Johnny? Why? Why not?

Notes:____

____

____

____

____

Task 5: Which of the adjectives below may be used to describe Johnny adequately? Defend your choice.

- ☐ upset
- ☐ happy
- ☐ hard-hearted
- ☐ caring
- ☐ desperate
- ☐ dangerous
- ☐ courageous
- ☐ unfeeling
- ☐ vulnerable
- ☐ cool

Task 6: Also taking into account the lyrics of "Desperado", re-watch the scene (0:58:48 – 1:00:48) and analyze it with regard to the connection between action and song. Does the song match the scene? Explain.

Notes:____

____

____

____

____

____

____

⌛____ minutes

The ending

Task 1: From the 16 words in the vocabulary box, choose 10 appropriate ones to fill in the gaps below. Then listen to the extract from the director's commentary (1:32:05 – 1:33:13) and check your answers.

"And in a way – you know at the end of the film – the father says goodbye to Frankie and it's pretty (1) ________________ – you know – I am kind of (2) __________________ to make my father say goodbye to him, but in a way I haven't (3) __________ done it, which is what the kind of end is about – or I haven't been (4) __________________, I have tried. I suppose you never can. But you can put it in (5) _________________________, I suppose. One of the things about this film with the men crying and all that is that a certain percentage of men find it hard to (6) __________________, because we're so used to the (7) __________________ god's story of the male who goes out and (8) _______________________ the world and is part of a (9) ____________. And this is more of a matriarchy: a man surrounded by women. The woman takes the active role in the procreation of life and sex and everything, and that freaks certain people out. And I say, "To hell with them!" – you know? It's like that's what I (10) ________________."

Vocabulary box

concentrate	together
hero	able
intended	dislike
punishes	patriarchy
deal with	perspective
warrior	odd
unlikely	saves
trying	even

Task 2: Discuss and comment on the goals Jim Sheridan wanted to achieve by shooting the ending the way he did.

⌛____ minutes

In America: Answer key

Viewing (worksheets 1a/1b, p. 12-13)

(1) Why did the family decide to come to the USA?
The family decided to come to the USA because of the death of their youngest son/brother Frankie. They want to leave their pain behind and hope for a new start in New York.

(2) How would you describe the first impression they get of New York?
The family is excited about the overwhelming and life-affirming atmosphere as they arrive at Times Square.

(3) What kind of housing does the family eventually reside in? How does Ariel refer to it?
They end up in a run-down apartment in Hell's Kitchen, one of the worst parts of New York. Ariel calls the house a "haunted house".

(4) Which (leit)motif recurs at the fun fair-scene?
Christy's "three whishes"-motif.

(5) Which character is introduced when Johnny is playing "Fee, fie, foe, fum..." with the children? Describe your first impression of this character.
The shot of Mateo depicts him as being physically threatening and mystical. According to critiques of the movie, this is also problematic since this impression of an African (American) man may reinforce the stereotype of the 'dark' (noble) savage.

(6) Johnny cannot "feel" the unborn baby? Why?
He has not yet recovered from the death of his son, Frankie. Johnny does not want to let go of the memory of Frankie. He feels that acknowledging the "new" child would result in the final loss of Frankie and of the memory of him.

(7) Sitting sick in his chair, what can be said about the disease Mateo is suffering from? What is special about the character of Ariel in this scene?
Mateo has contracted HIV and eventually dies of the disease. Ariel is not scared when she approaches Mateo. She shows the innocence typical of a child her age. This innocence seems so noble that – as the director might have wanted to suggest – everybody should take notice and behave the same way.

(8) What is the symbolism inherent in cutting back and forth between the rapping stockbroker and the lifeless Mateo?
This parallel editing (also: cross-cutting) criticizes the superficiality of the rich who take drugs (cocaine) for fun. The drug-induced behavior of the stockbroker is juxtaposed with the image of Mateo, a human being dying from HIV, which, after all, is also known for being transmitted by infected syringes used by drug addicts.

(9) What happens when Mateo dies?
A metaphor suggested by parallel editing shows that at the moment Mateo dies, the new-born is brought back to life. This might also be seen as problematic since the character of Mateo has sacrificed his life for the survival of the baby. He does not seem to be a character in his own right, but rather the embodiment of a noble savage.

Movie synopsis (worksheet 2, p. 14)

(1) enter (2) headed (3) recover (4) tends (5) waits (6) dare (7) befriends (8) gives (9) save (10) dies (11) paid (12) strengthened

Expert Groups (Worksheets 3a-6b)

Expert group 1: Jack and the Beanstalk (worksheets 3a-3c, p. 15-17)

Check the following website for answers:

- http://en.wikipedia.org/wiki/Jack_and_the_Beanstalk

Expert group 2: Halloween (worksheets 4a/4b, p. 18-19)

Check the following website for answers:

- http://www.historychannel.com/exhibits/halloween

Expert group 3: Narrative perspective (worksheets (5a/5b, p. 20-21)

The narrative perspective as conveyed by Christy through her camcorder and via voice-overs depicts part of the movie from her subjective point of view. Christy's narration, however subjective, contains elaborate insights. She seems to act as the family's guardian, protecting the family with her three wishes. At one point in the movie she even takes over the role of the mother. For a child her age, Christy seems to be very mature – maybe even too mature for her own good. Mourning silently, she carries the burden of unresolved grief over the death of Frankie, her brother. Ariel, on the other hand, strikes the viewer as carefree and innocent. She is a very inquisitive girl and her straightforward questions are the source of many humorous dialogues in the movie. If she was to narrate the voice-over for the fun fair-scene, her approach would be much more childlike and innocent – also marked by a simpler choice of words and syntactic structures. She would probably be disappointed in her father for initially failing to win an E.T.-doll for her. Unlike Christy, she might not be able to perceive the consequences that would result from losing all the family's money.

Expert group 4: Music (worksheets 6a/6b, p. 22-23)

(1) out riding fences
(2) laid upon your table
(3) is your best bet
(4) the queen of diamonds
(5) things that are pleasing you
(6) a rainbow above you
(7) come to your senses
(8) let somebody love you
(9) the ones you can't get
(10) you have got your reasons

This scene is partly filmed through Christy's camcorder, operated this time by her father. The song "Desperado" tells the story of a man *desperate* to find happiness. This man, although kind at heart, has a tendency to put himself and others at risk by thoughtless behavior and actions. From the way the scene is shot, it is clear that the song is addressed to Johnny, who shares many of the characteristics of the man in the song. Christy seems to plead with her father to get over the loss of his son, Frankie, – as indicated by the flashbacks via camcorder –, to stop living in the past, to return to the present, and be there for the family. The atmosphere in this scene can be described as very emotional. Christy and Johnny seem to be in a direct dialogue. Although in public, theirs is a very private moment.

The Ending (worksheet 7, p. 24)

(1) odd (2) trying (3) even (4) able to (5) perspective (6) deal with (7) warrior (8) challenges (9) patriarchy (10) intended

Zum Film

Der Film *Whale Rider*, der im Jahre 2002 in die Kinos kam, ist ein Geheimtipp unter den hier vorgestellten Filmen. Regie führte die neuseeländische Regisseurin Niki Caro. Der Film fokussiert die neuseeländische Minorität der Maori und entfernt sich dabei kulturell von der vorherrschenden Konzentration auf Großbritannien bzw. die USA. Zudem ist der Film inhaltlich wie filmtechnisch ein ansprechendes cineastisches Werk. *Whale Rider* bietet eine Aufnahme aktueller Konzepte der *cultural studies* vor allem in Bezug auf Minoritäten.

DVD cover

Der Film beruht auf einer Buchvorlage des Schriftstellers Sir Witi Tahe Ihimaera (Maori) und gibt – ähnlich wie der Roman *The Whale Rider* (1987) – Einblicke in die Kultur, die Traditionen und die Geschichte der Maori. Der Film spricht zudem aus der Kultur der Maori *heraus*; das heißt, er bietet nicht die übliche Außensicht auf eine „andere“ und zudem indigene Kultur, sondern vermittelt eine Innensicht. Diese ermöglicht es den Lernenden, die Kultur und Lebensweise der Maori heute aus erster Hand zu erfahren. Dabei wird die Kultur der Maori nicht als exotisch dargestellt oder gar der Eindruck erweckt, dass es sich hier um einen alternativen Lebensentwurf im Gegensatz zur „westlichen“ Kultur handeln soll. Vielmehr vermag der Film die Universalien zwischen allen Kulturen anzusprechen. Die Protagonistin Paikea (Keisha Castle-Hughes) befindet sich in einer Sinnkrise, die ähnlich wie in allen Kulturen – und damit auch in der deutschen – dadurch ausgelöst wird, dass sich Jugendliche im Konflikt mit der Eltern- bzw. der Großelterngeneration befinden. Folgendes *voice-over*, das den Film in der *opening scene* einleitet, verdeutlicht diesen Konflikt:

> In the old days, the land felt a great emptiness. It was waiting to be filled up, waiting for someone to love it, waiting for a leader. And he came on the back of a whale meant to lead a new people. Our ancestor Paikea. But now we were waiting for the first-born of a new generation, for the descendant of the Whale Rider, for the boy who would be chief. [...] But he died. And I didn't. My Koro wished in his heart that I'd never been born. But he changed his mind.

In der Tradition der Maori ist es für ein weibliches Mitglied der Gemeinschaft nicht möglich, die Rolle eines Oberhauptes für die Maori-Gemeinde zu übernehmen. Ihimaera selbst betont in einem Interview (enthalten im Extramaterial der DVD) jedoch auch den universellen Wert der Geschichte Paikeas: „I hope that every young girl in the world embraces this story. It's their own, because they have so many challenges to face.“

So lässt der Film die Legende von Paikea, dem Walreiter, wiederaufleben. Diese ist vor allem im neuseeländischen Whangara, dem Schauplatz der Filmhandlung, eine zentrale Herkunftsgeschichte der dort ansässigen Maori. Die Legende besagt, dass der Urahne Paikea einst auf dem Rücken eines Wals auf Aotearoa, dem Namen der Maori für Neuseeland, gestrandet sei.

Auch der Autor Ihimaera erinnerte sich an das Symbol des Wals, welches ihm durch ein besonderes Erlebnis in New York in das Gedächtnis gerufen wurde:

> In 1989, I was living in New York on the 33rd floor of an apartment building and all of the sudden I heard these helicopters around the building. [...] When I looked out I saw that there was this whale. This whale had arrived right there, halfway up the Hudson River. It was the most amazing occurrence. My thoughts turned to Whangara and to all of those wonderful whale stories that I had heard from my boyhood – and in particular the story of Paikea, who came from Hawaiki to New Zealand on the back of a whale.

Der Film war ein großer Publikumserfolg. Er gewann den Toronto International Film Festival AGF Peoples Choice Award (2002) und den Sundance Film Festival World Cinema Audience Award (2003). Die damals elfjährige Schauspielerin Keisha Castle-Hughes, die zuvor noch keine Schauspielerfahrung hatte, wurde zudem für einen Academy Award als Beste Schauspielerin nominiert. Sie spielt neben so etablierten neuseeländischen Schauspielern wie Cliff Curtis (Porourangi) und Rawiri Paratene (Koro).

Zur Durchführung der Unterrichtsreihe

Dieser bereits für die Klassen 9 und 10 einsetzbare Film (97 Minuten, ab 6 Jahren) sollte aufgrund seines emotionalen Gehalts in einer Sitzung in Gänze gesehen werden. Ist eine Sequenzialisierung notwendig, so sollte der Film höchstens in zwei Abschnitte unterteilt werden. Flexibel adaptierbare Zeitrahmen für die Bearbeitung der Arbeitsblätter sind dem Inhaltsverzeichnis zu entnehmen.

Als Einstieg könnte als *pre-viewing task* ein Ausschnitt aus dem Roman *The Whale Rider* (Ausgabe von B&T, 2003) stehen. Gleichermaßen bietet es sich immer an, anhand eines DVD-Covers oder eines Filmposters (www.impawards.com) mit den Lernenden über den Inhalt des Films zu spekulieren. Am Anfang könnte auch eine Auseinandersetzung mit der Machart des Trailers stehen, der im Extramaterial der DVD enthalten ist.

Da der Film *Whale Rider* von der Dynamik zwischen seinen Protagonisten lebt, wird das Augenmerk zunächst auf diese und deren Entwicklung innerhalb des Films gerichtet. Ein erstes Arbeitsblatt (WS 1a), das filmbegleitend, aber auch in der Rückschau auf ausgewählte Szenen eingesetzt werden kann, verdeutlicht die Entwicklung der komplex gezeichneten, mehrdimensionalen Charaktere (*round characters*) und soll sowohl Sprechanlässe als auch Möglichkeiten zur Reaktivierung von Vokabeln bieten.

Der so gewonnene Einblick in die Motivationen der Charaktere kann in einer zweiten Aufgabe in ein Diagramm umgesetzt werden (WS 1b), welches die verschiedenen Konflikte zwischen den Charakteren grafisch verdeutlichen soll. Hierbei kann den Schülern einerseits freie Hand gegeben werden, andererseits könnte eine Vorgabe – wie etwa die Platzierung Koros im Zentrum des Diagramms – den Einstieg in diese Teamarbeit erleichtern. In einem weiteren Schritt soll verdeutlicht werden, wie sehr die Konflikte zwischen den Charakteren durch ihre Existenz *zwischen* zwei Kulturen geprägt werden. Die vorgegebene Grafik kann dabei in einer Klassendiskussion als Tafelbild vervollständigt werden. Das Arbeitsblatt zur *movie synopsis* (WS 2) verbindet die nochmalige Zusammenfassung des Plots mit einer Aufgabe, bei der die Lernenden die Filmzusammenfassung aus Fragmenten kohärent rekonstruieren müssen.

Es folgt eine Auseinandersetzung mit zentralen Themen des Films *Whale Rider* in Gruppenarbeit (WS 3): (1) *leadership*, (2) *gender roles*, (3) *achievement*, (4) *working together*. Diese Themen werden mit kreativen Arbeitsaufträgen verbunden, die in Gruppenarbeit zur Produktion von verschiedenen Textsorten (Stellengesuch, Brief, Rede, *voice-over* zum Filmtrailer) führen sollen.

Die Miteinbeziehung mediendidaktischer Überlegungen wird zunächst durch eine filmerzählerische Aufgabe eingeleitet (WS 4), in der sich die Lernenden mit zwei zentralen Motiven auseinandersetzen, die als Metaphern im Film fungieren. Des Weiteren wird eine detaillierte Analyse einer Filmszene dazu genutzt (WS 5), den Lernenden ausgewähltes filmsprachliches Vokabular vorab terminologisch zu vermitteln und so die detaillierte Interpretation einer Szene zu ermöglichen.

Eine weitere ausgewählte Filmszene ist dann Teil einer Höraufgabe, die zunächst als *cloze excercise* dient (WS 6). Die Hör- bzw. Vokabelaufgabe stellt die Rede der Protagonistin Paikea in den Mittelpunkt, weil diese nicht nur einen besonderen emotionalen Gehalt hat, sondern auch Auskunft über den zentralen Mythos der Maori vom Walreiter Paikea gibt. Hier bietet sich zudem Anlass zur Diskussion, da Paikea mit ihrer Rede eine Neudefinition der Figur „Paikea“ erreicht. Sie sieht Paikea nicht mehr als alleinige Führungsfigur, wie sie sich noch in ihrem Großvater Koro verkörpert, sondern als eine Figur, die nur fest in die Gemeinde integriert und mit deren Hilfe Führungspotenzial entwickeln kann.

In kreativer sowie produktions- und handlungsorientierter Hinsicht bietet ein Arbeitsblatt zum *storyboarding* den Lernenden die Möglichkeit, einmal selbst ein *storyboard* anzufertigen und so einen Einblick in eine bestimmte Phase der Produktion von Filmen zu erhalten (WS 7a/7b). Neben dem Filmskript ist das *storyboard* ein weiterer wichtiger Zwischenschritt in der Produktion von Filmen. Hier ergibt sich zudem die Gelegenheit, das zuvor vermittelte filmtechnische Vokabular nochmals anzuwenden und zu erweitern. Die Lernenden werden so dazu angeregt, über die Wirkung bestimmter Einstellungen nachzudenken und zu diskutieren.

Abschließend wird in einem Beispiel für eine WebQuest die Aufgabe gestellt, gezieltes Wissen über ausgewählte Termini aus der Sprache der Maori und deren Hintergrund zu sammeln (WS 8a/8b). Dieses Beispiel gibt eine Struktur vor, die als Paradigma auch für weitere WebQuests genutzt werden kann: (1) Einführung, (2) allgemeine Aufgabenstellung, (3) konkrete Fragen, (4) vorgegebene Internetquellen, (5) Hinweise zur Präsentation und Bewertung. Weitere Themen können so in einer WebQuest als Gruppenarbeit abgedeckt werden: (1) der Paikea-Mythos, (2) heilige Symbole der Maori, (3) die Baustruktur und Bedeutung des *marae* (meeting place) oder des *waka* (canoe), (4) charakteristische Tattoos der Maori, (5) die Maori heute, (6) Sport – die All Blacks, das neuseeländische Rugby-Team, (7) Geografie, Politik, Geschichte. Als Anlaufpunkte für diese WebQuests können neben www.wikipedia.org, www.reference.com oder www.answers.com folgende Quellen dienen:

- http://maaori.com
- http://www.maori.org.nz
- http://www.teara/govt.nz/NewZealanders/en

Die WebQuest rundet die Auseinandersetzung mit dem Film *Whale Rider* ab. Sie bietet dabei die Möglichkeit der eigenen Recherche und der kreativen Präsentation der Ergebnisse.

Main characters

Task 1: Choose one of the five main characters (Koro, Flowers, Paikea, Porourangi, Rawiri) and trace his/her development throughout the movie. Use the table below as a guideline for your answers.

Character: ____________________

	Actions & behavior	Interaction with other characters	Motivation
Beginning			
Middle			
End			

___ minutes

Whale Rider: Worksheet 1b

Task 2: Create a diagram in which you outline the relationship(s) between the characters and the conflicts between them.

Task 3: Where would you position each character in the diagram below? Why?

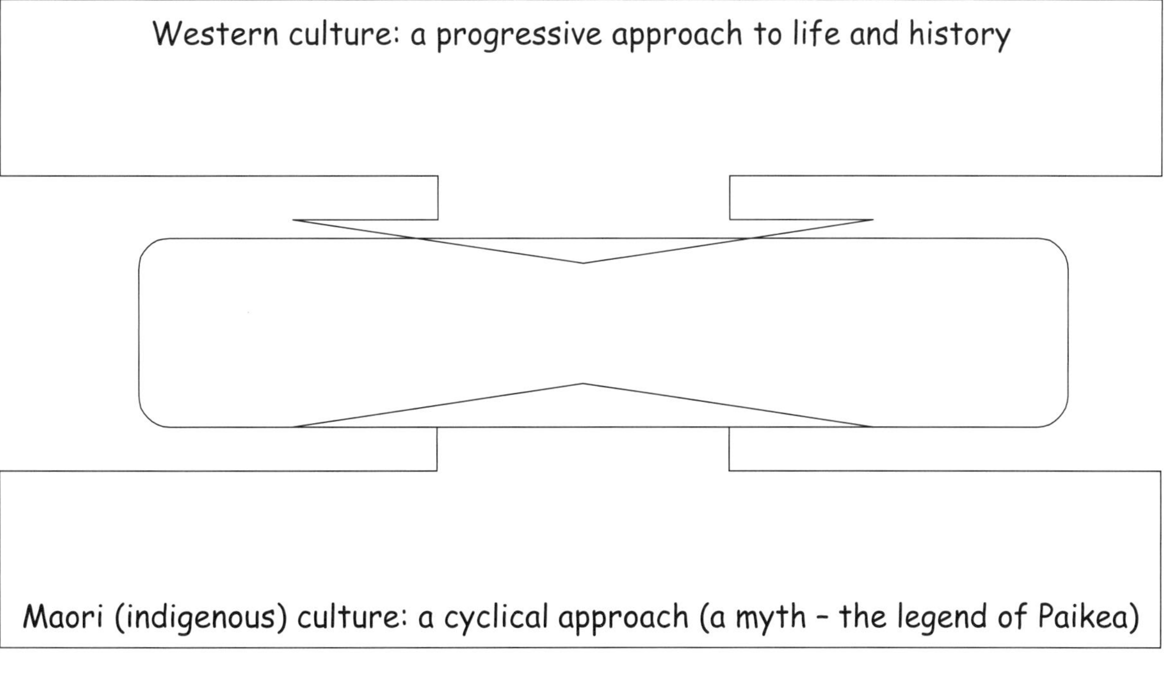

⌛___ minutes

Movie synopsis

Task: The movie synopsis has been jumbled up. Put the paragraphs back into the right order.

(1) After Paikea had nearly died rescuing the whales, the movie cuts to the hospital where we witness Koro worshipping the unconscious Paikea as the new leader of his people.

(2) When a shoal of whales is washed upon shore unable to move back into the ocean, Paikea can prove her strength once again.

(3) In order to find the new chief among the boys, Koro has set up a special school for all the first-born boys from the village. There he wants to teach them the skills and knowledge it takes to be a Maori leader.

(4) Koro has finally accepted that his granddaughter will be the new chief of the Maori community.

(5) Paikea's mother dies during labor and with her Paikea's twin brother, who was meant to be the future chief. According to a Maori legend, the first-born son of a generation is meant to be chief.

(6) While the entire village rushes to the shore to help the whales move back into the ocean, it is Paikea, who is able to rescue the whales.

(7) Their relationship deteriorates because Koro is so focused on finding the new chief among the boys that he does not realize that Paikea is the one destined to be the new leader. He does not want her to interfere with the traditional ways. When Paikea is the one retrieving the whale tooth which Koro used to wear around his neck from the ocean, the audience realizes that Paikea is meant to be the next chief and that she has passed the ultimate test. However, it still takes another test of Paikea's strength to convince Koro.

(8) Koro, the present chief, is determined to carry on this tradition, trying to prevent Paikea from becoming chief because she is a girl.

(9) Paikea is not allowed to attend this school. She tries in vain to gain acceptance and respect from her grandfather. The more Paikea tries to impress Koro, the more he gets upset about her.

Answer: _ _ _ _ _ _ _ _ _

⌛___ minutes

Whale Rider: Worksheet 3

Central themes

Task: As a group, choose one of the themes below. Discuss where and how it is touched upon in the movie. Then complete the creative writing task.

Theme: Leadership

Create a leadership job specification that outlines the qualities you are looking for in an excellent leader.

Theme: Gender roles

Write a letter to Koro to try and persuade him to change his views about women not meant to become leaders.

Theme: Achievement

Write a short speech in which Rawiri addresses the Maori community summoned at the shore to rescue the whales.

Theme: Working together

With a focus on your theme, write a new voice-over for the trailer of the movie Whale Rider.

⌛____ minutes

Central motifs

Task: Analyze and discuss the meaning of two motifs – the rope and the waka. How do these motifs function as metaphors in the movie?

Koro shows Paikea the rope

The rope:____________________________

The waka:____________________________

The unfinished waka *at the shore*

____ minutes

A powerful scene

Task 1: Describe the use of "movie language" in the following powerful scene at the hospital (0:01:11 - 0:03:12). Re-watch the scene and tick the effects that you think are used.

- ☐ slow motion
- ☐ high-angle shot
- ☐ fast-cutting
- ☐ Dutch angle
- ☐ split screen
- ☐ parallel editing
- ☐ long shot
- ☐ flashback
- ☐ over-the-shoulder shot
- ☐ voice-over
- ☐ extreme close-up

Paikea's mother in labor

Task 2: In a few sentences, describe how these effects support the special atmosphere of the scene.

Description: ____

____ minutes

Paikea's speech

Task 1: Fill in the gaps in Paikea's speech below with words from the vocabulary box. Check your answers when you listen to the speech (1:08:49 - 1:12:29) afterwards.

This speech is a (1) _________ of my deep love and respect for Koro Apirana – my grandfather. My name is Paikea Apirana ... and I come from a long line of (2) __________ stretching all the way back to Hawaiki, where our ancient ones are. The ones that first heard the man crying in sentiment. His name was also Paikea ... and I am the most recent (3) ____________. But I was not the leader my grandfather was expecting and by being born I broke the line back to the (4) _____________ ones. It wasn't anybody's fault – it just happened. [cut to Koro – long pause] But we can learn and if the knowledge is given to everyone then we can have lots of leaders and soon everyone will be strong, not just the ones that have been chosen. Because sometimes – even if you're the leader and you need to be strong, you can get tired ... like our (5) ___________ Paikea when he was lost at sea and he couldn't find the land and he probably wanted to die. But he knew the ancient ones were there for him so he called out to them to lift him up and give him strength. This is his (6) ______________________. I (7) _______________ it to my grandfather.

Vocabulary box
chant: a song or melody
ancient: dating from a remote period
token: something representing something else (facts, events, feelings)
chiefs: the head or ruler of a tribe or clan
ancestor: a person from one whom is descended, a forefather
dedicate: to devote wholly and earnestly, as to some person or purpose
descendant: a person that is descended from a specific ancestor

Task 2: Which message regarding leadership does Paikea want to convey with her speech? Elaborate.

⌛___ minutes

Storyboarding

ⓘ Storyboard

A series of frames (drawings) which depict a sequence in a movie shot by shot. Storyboards illustrate a shot/frame and include both a sketch and a technical description of the shot/frame. Storyboards are meant to give directors an idea of how the film will look when it is finished.

Task 1: Read the excerpt from the book The Whale Rider below.

Astride the whale she felt the sting of the surf and rain upon her face. Either side the younger whales were escorting the leader through the surf. They broke through into deeper water. Her heart was pounding. She saw now she was surrounded by the whale herd. Every now and then, one of the whales would come to rub alongside the ancient leader. (Whale Rider: 129)

Task 2: Use the above excerpt and "translate" it into single frames. Before you start, have a look at the sample frame below. It was created by a student for the first (underlined) sentence of the excerpt. Create your own storyboard on the next page. Draw the frames in the left-hand column and note the effects you used in the right-hand column.

Student's sample storyboard

Storyboard

Frame	Sketch	Effects / Explanation
1		
2		
3		
4		

Task 3: Compare your storyboard with the actual scene in the movie and the director's audio commentary (1:24:46 - 1:27:35). Discuss differences.

⌛___ minutes

Whale Rider: Worksheet 8a

WebQuest: Maori terms and traditions

Introduction:
Your group is asked to gather information on one Maori term and the tradition that goes along with it.

A hongi: traditional Maori greeting between men

General Task:
In your search, complete the tasks on this and the next page by accessing the websites provided.

Task 1: As a team, choose one of the terms below. Translate the term by accessing http://www.maoridictionary.co.nz and match the word with an appropriate picture.

☐ haka:____________________

☐ waka:____________________

☐ marae:____________________

- ☐ taiaha:________________

- ☐ paikea:________________

Task 2: As a team, find out more about the term you have chosen. Type your term into the search engine at:

- www.wikipedia.org

Notes:____

____

____

____

____

____

____

Task 3: Design a presentation in order to share your information with the class. Use an appropriate scene from the movie to illustrate your presentation.

haka: 1:31:30 - 1:32:00
waka: 1:32:15 - 1:33:45
marae: 0:33:49 - 0:35:20
taiaha: 0:37:05 - 0:38:05
paikea: 0:10:00 - 0:11:19

⌛___ minutes

Whale Rider: Answer key

Main characters

Character development (worksheet 1a, p. 30)

All of the characters in the movie *Whale Rider* show a development throughout the movie. Their actions, thoughts, and interactions with other characters give evidence to this effect.

Koro, for example, changes from being a loving grandfather into an increasingly stubborn chief. Yet, at the end of the movie he worships Paikea and has found his peace with her becoming the new chief. Koro has finally accepted that his granddaughter will be the new chief, and with that acceptance the entire Maori community transforms from a state of stasis and melancholy into one of triumph, cherishing the renewal and revitalization of Maori tradition.

Nanny Flowers, Koro's wife, is a very strong and outspoken woman. At the beginning of the movie she even threatens Koro with a divorce, when he is unwilling to accept his granddaughter Paikea. Throughout the movie she is very caring. She comforts Paikea and is persistent in trying to convince Koro that his ideals are outdated, that change is inevitable.

Porourangi, Paikea's father, is shown as very insecure, especially when he is around his father. He had left the family and Paikea after the death of his wife and son and is now caught between two worlds. His modern art photography is juxtaposed with the traditional *waka*, which he left behind unfinished. When he fails at taking Paikea with him to the city, he tries hard to come to grips with his feeling of non-belonging. At the end of the movie, however, his *waka* has been refurbished and Porourangi is reintegrated into the Maori community. Even his German girlfriend, Anna, standing at the shore with the Maori community, is welcome.

Rawiri, Porourangi's younger brother, is introduced as a very young boy, who – like Paikea – seems to have suffered from his father's strong-headed adherence to tradition, especially regarding the role of the male in the Maori community. Grown up, Rawiri is shown as an obese and apparently unemployed man. He hangs out with his friends and girlfriend. However, when he teaches Paikea the arts of traditional Maori stick-fighting, we learn that Rawiri used to be a master with the *taiaha*. Upon that moment Rawiri grows more and more determined, trying to get back into shape. At the end of the movie, he even leads the Maori community in their fight to rescue the shoal of whales beached at the shore.

Paikea refuses to adhere to her grandfather's traditional ways. She is the lead in a school play and is introduced as a very intelligent and inquisitive girl. When Koro opens up his school for boys, she tries in vain to gain acceptance and respect from her grandfather. She practices *mai rakau*, Maori stick fighting, with her uncle Rawiri, she learns ancient Maori chants, prayers, calls, tribal lore, and warrior techniques. However, the more Paikea tries to impress Koro, the more he gets upset about her. When Paikea gives her speech in honor of her grandfather, she is heartbroken because of his absence. However, when Paikea is the one retrieving the whale tooth from the ocean, Koro has to accept that Paikea is meant to be the next chief. Thereupon, she rescues the whales and finally sits center stage next to her grandfather in the *waka*.

Relationship(s) and conflicts (worksheet 1b, p. 31)
A graph outlining the relationship(s) with a focus on the conflicts between the characters may look like this:

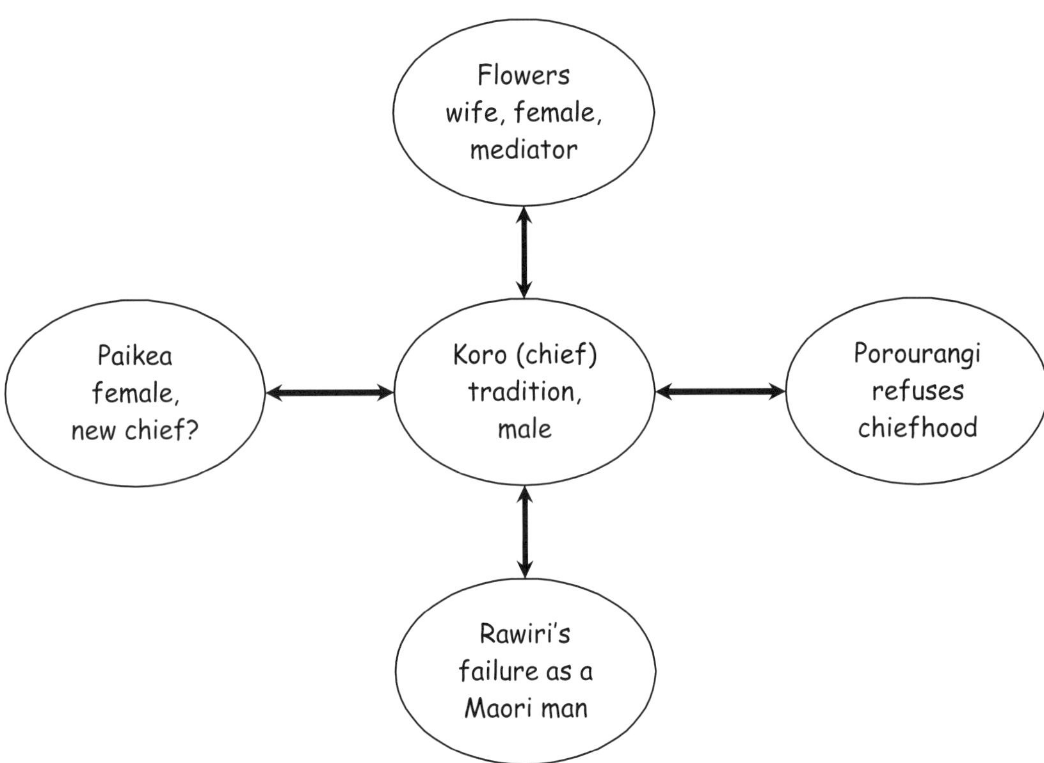

Movie synopsis (worksheet 2, p. 32)

Answer: 5 8 3 9 7 2 6 1 4

Central motifs (worksheet 4, p. 34)

The rope:
Koro uses the rope as a metaphor to teach Paikea about Maori history and about how the community consists of little threads, which are important to make a strong rope as well as a strong community. The rope breaks when he tries to start the engine. This may symbolize the extent to which the local Maori community has recently been disintegrating, how individuals have become weak (alcoholics, unemployed, lazy, etc.), and how this has caused the entire community to lose its strength. The rope features once again at the end of the movie when the community is trying to rescue the whales. Here the rope does not hold the whale and breaks once again. However, in the scene with her grandfather Paikea was able to fix the rope and start the engine. This shows that Paikea can be reinvigorating for the community, giving it a new and fresh start. She is the one who rescues the whales.

Whale Rider: Answer key

The waka:

Unfinished at the beginning of the movie, the *waka* is another symbol for the community's disintegration. It has been left behind by Porourangi, who himself has left behind his community and ancient traditions to start anew in the city. However, throughout the movie many scenes take place in the *waka*. Porourangi comforts his daughter Paikea in the *waka*. Paikea leads from the *waka*, singing traditional Maori chants and calling the whales. At the end of the movie, the *waka* gracefully moves into the picture. It has been refurbished. The Maori community is united in the *waka* as a symbol for the community's revival, apparently moving into a brighter future.

A powerful scene (worksheet 5, p. 35)

The movie starts with a narrative of Paikea's birth. The "movie language" used in this scene ranges from **voice-over-techniques** to **(extreme) close-ups**. These show minute detail and convey the massive pain Paikea's mother is going through during labor. Shots through a **blurred lense**, **slow motion** and the use of a **Dutch angle** (canted angle) add force to the eerie atmosphere of this scene. **Parallel editing** – cuts back and forth between the act of birth and the whales underwater – creates a metaphorical link between Paikea's birth and the story of the whale rider Paikea. A **high angle shot** down on Porourangi caressing his dead wife suggests vulnerability and loneliness.

Paikea's speech (worksheet 6, p. 36)

Paikea redefines the role of a leader. She does not expect from a leader to be the strongest in the community. She thinks that only the support of the community will make a leader strong. In a voice-over at the end of the movie Paikea utters this message once again: "I'm not a prophet, but I know that our people will keep going forward – all together, with all of our strength."

(1) token (2) chiefs (3) ancient (4) descendant (5) knowledge (6) strong (7) ancestor

WebQuest: Maori terms and traditions (worksheets 8a/8b, p. 39-40)

Picture 1 - *waka* (canoe):

- a Maori watercraft used for fishing, river travel, or oceanic voyages. A large *waka* may be manned by up to 80 paddlers.

Picture 2 - *haka* (a dance):

- a Maori posture dance accompanied by singing and shouting. The *haka* is performed by a group (of men or women). They are performed for various reasons.

Picture 3 - *marae* (meeting place):

- the enclosed space in front of a *wharenui* (meeting house). The *marae* is a sacred place serving religious and social purposes.

Picture 4 - *paikea* (whale/whale rider):

- the name of an ancestor of the *Ngāti Porou*, a Maori tribe of the east coast of New Zealand's North Island. The name was assumed by *Kahutia-te-rangi* because he was assisted by humpback whales (*paikea*) to survive an attempt on his life by his half-brother Ruatapu.

Picture 5 - *taiaha* (fighting stick):

- a wooden weapon used as a close quarter's weapon for short, sharp strikes during stick fighting. It is one of the weapons used for *mau rakau* (Maori martial arts).

Zum Film

Der Film *Bend It Like Beckham* (112 Minuten, ab 6 Jahren) ist mittlerweile bereits ein Schulklassiker. In den Lehr- und Rahmenplänen einiger Bundesländer wird der Film konkret für den Einsatz in der Schule vorgeschlagen. Dabei sollte aber nicht vergessen werden, dass er auf einer Romanvorlage beruht, die sich thematisch, sprachlich und den Umfang betreffend ebenso für die Schule eignet. Buch und Film können – im Schwierigkeitsgrad entsprechend abgestimmt und didaktisiert – nicht nur in der Sekundarstufe II eingesetzt werden, sondern bereits in den Klassen 9 oder 10. Diese Kompatibilität ergibt sich einerseits aus der für dieses Lernalter sprachlich angemessenen Romanvorlage, die als annotierte Schullektüre unter anderem vom Klett Verlag vorliegt, andererseits auch aus der thematischen Vielfalt, die sowohl der Text als auch der Film bieten.

DVD cover

Themen wie Generations- und Kulturkonflikte, Rollenerwartungen, Liebe und Freundschaft, Homosexualität und nicht zuletzt das Thema des interkulturellen Verstehens und Lernens werden durch den Film angesprochen und problematisiert. Dabei gewährt der Umstand, dass beide Protagonistinnen sich im Alter der Lernenden befinden und mitunter ähnliche Probleme haben dürften wie sie, die Möglichkeit, auf den Erfahrungshorizont der Lernenden zurückzugreifen und damit ein hohes Identifikations- und Motivationspotenzial zu generieren. Die Darstellung zweier Initiationsgeschichten von Mädchen aus unterschiedlichen Kulturkreisen zeigt dabei mehr Gemeinsamkeiten als Unterschiede, was letztlich auch dazu beiträgt, das vielfältige Angebot der in den Film eingebrachten Probleme aufzunehmen und zu ergründen.

Die Lernenden werden in die Lage versetzt, Sympathie und Empathie für eine oder mehrere der Figuren zu empfinden. Dies wiederum wird es Lehrenden erleichtern, interkulturelle Kompetenzen in den Unterricht mit einzubeziehen und zu vermitteln, denn interkulturelles Verständnis entsteht aus der Fähigkeit zum Perspektivenwechsel, zur Perspektivenübernahme und zur Perspektivenkoordinierung (der Reflexion auf die persönliche Lebenssituation). Hier kommt hinzu, dass beide Protagonistinnen bekannt sind bzw. zunehmend bekannter werden. Parminder Nagra (Jessminder) ist zurzeit vor allem als Dr. Neela Rasgotra aus der amerikanischen Serie *Emergency Room* bekannt. Keira Knightley (Jules) ist neben ihren Rollen in *Star Wars – Episode I: The Phantom Menace* (1999) und dem britischer Thriller *The Hole* (2001) vor allem für ihre Rolle neben Johnny Depp in *Pirates of the Carribean* (2003, 2006) berühmt geworden.

Das Extramaterial auf der DVD *Bend It Like Beckham* bietet neben interessanten Hintergrunddaten zur Entstehung des Films auch Informationen zur Autobiografie der Regisseurin Gurinder Chadha. Diese gab mit *Bhaji on the Beach* (1993) ihr Regiedebüt. Diesem Film folgten thematisch ähnlich gelagerte Filme anderer Regisseure, wie etwa Damian O'Donnells *East Is East* (1999) und Mira Nairs *Monsoon Wedding* (2001). Während diese Filme zum Teil einen weitaus tragischeren Zugang zum Thema des inter- wie intrakulturellen Konflikts wählen, zeigt sich *Bend It Like Beckham* als Kömodie, die zudem mit den filmischen Traditionen Bollywoods spielt. Zahllose Witze und Spitzen gegen die eigene und die britische Kultur leuchten nicht nur den Kulturkonflikt aus, sondern verhandeln auch stereotype Geschlechterrollen neu. Termini wie „gora“ (abwertend: weißer Engländer), „paki“ (abwertend: Angehörige(r) der pakistanischen Gemeinde) oder „butch“ (abwertend: Mädchen/Frau mit maskulinen Zügen) werden im Film verwendet. Sie verdeutlichen die menschliche Tendenz, komplexe Sachverhalte über Stereotype zu vereinfachen, um diese so besser in die eigenen Verstehenskategorien integrierbar zu machen. Walter Lippman hat in seiner richtungweisenden und grundlegenden Studie *Public Opinion* (1922) über die Bildung von Stereotypen folgende Ausführungen gemacht:

> A pattern of stereotypes is not neutral. It is not merely a way of substituting order for the great blooming, buzzing confusion of reality. It is not merely a shortcut. [...] It is the guarantee of our self-respect; it is the projection upon the world of our own sense, of our own value, our own position and our own rights. The stereotypes are, therefore, highly charged with the feelings that are attached to them. They are the fortress of our tradition, and behind its defenses we can continue to feel ourselves safe in the position we occupy. (Lippman, Walter. New York: Free Press, 1965, 63-64)

Vor diesem Hintergrund will die vorgeschlagene Unterrichtsreihe eine Grundlage für die Diskussion von Vorurteilsstrukturen bieten, die Lernende auch in der Reflexion auf sich selbst und ihr soziales Umfeld verhandeln können.

Zur Durchführung der Unterrichtsreihe

Flexibel adaptierbare Zeitrahmen für die Bearbeitung der Arbeitsblätter sind wiederum dem Inhaltsverzeichnis zu entnehmen. Am Anfang der Sequenz steht die Arbeit mit Filmpostern als konkreter Einstieg in die Unterrichtsreihe (WS 1). Die Poster, die hier nicht abgedruckt werden konnten, sollten in der Vorbereitung durch die Lehrenden entsprechend kopiert bzw. vervielfältigt werden (die Farbkopie auf Folie bietet sich an). Sie sind auf folgenden Webseiten zu erhalten:

- http://www.impawards.com/2003/bend_it_like_beckham_ver2.html (GB)
- http://www.impawards.com/2003/bend_it_like_beckham_ver3.html (USA)

Die Arbeit mit Filmpostern bietet vielfältige Möglichkeiten der Diskussion. Zunächst kann über das Thema des Films spekuliert werden. Des Weiteren können die Lernenden ihre eigene Bewertung der Poster zur Diskussion stellen. Zum anderen wird im Rahmen der Intertextualität die Beschreibung einer weiteren Textsorte aufgenommen, welche den Lernenden aus ihrem alltäglichen Freizeitleben bekannt ist. Es bietet sich die Möglichkeit, über die Aufmachung von Filmpostern zu diskutieren. Diese werden ja letztlich konzipiert, um Zuschauern die Attraktivität des Films zu vermitteln und sie in den Film zu „locken“. Zudem stammen die zwei vorgeschlagenen Poster aus verschiedenen Kulturkreisen – dem britischen einerseits und dem amerikanischen andererseits. Auch dieser Umstand könnte vor dem Hintergrund der unterschiedlicher Farbgebung, verschiedener *strap lines*, und sprachlicher Details diskutiert werden.

Im weiteren Verlauf der Unterrichtsreihe wird eine Sequenzialisierung des Films in vier Sequenzen vorgeschlagen. Jede Sequenz ist etwa 20 Minuten lang und betont verschiedene im Film aufgeworfene Themen.

Die erste Sequenz und das entsprechende Arbeitsblatt bietet einen konkreten Diskussionsanlass (WS 2), indem die im Film dargestellten Geschlechterrollen (dabei vor allem die weibliche) thematisiert werden. Die Schülerinnen aber auch die Schüler werden in einem zweiten Schritt dazu aufgefordert, über ihre eigenen Erfahrungen zum Thema Geschlechterrollen in ihrem eigenen (nicht immer deutschen) Kulturkreis zu sprechen.

Die zweite Sequenz verfolgt das Ziel, die Vielschichtigkeit der im Film aufgezeigten Konflikte zu erläutern. Die Konfliktsituation ist nicht allein nur auf den vermeintlichen Gegensatz zwischen indischer und britischer Kultur ausgelegt, sondern zeigt auch die vielfältigen intrakulturellen Konflikte auf (WS 3).

In der dritten Sequenz werden die Lernenden direkt zum Perspektivenwechsel motiviert (WS 4a/4b). Vor dem Hintergrund eines *crucial incident* für Jessminder sollen die Lernenden Jessminders Emotionen über Adjektive definieren, die entsprechend ausgewählt werden müssen. Im weiteren Verlauf soll der Perspektivenwechsel über einen selbst verfassten Tagebucheintrag realisiert werden. Um diese Aufgabenstellung auch für die männlichen Lernenden zu erleichtern, wird vorgeschlagen, die Schülerinnen aus der Perspektive Jessminders schreiben zu lassen, während die Schüler sich mit der Perspektive Joes, des Trainers, auseinandersetzen.

Die vierte Sequenz fokussiert die Hauptaussage des Films, die wie folgt lauten könnte: „Alles ist zu erreichen." Oder: „Lass' dich durch nichts aufhalten." Diese Hauptaussage wird durch eine kurze Rede von Jessminders Vater dargeboten (WS 5). In Verbindung mit einer späteren Diskussion bietet sich hier eine Höraufgabe an, die das Einsetzen der entsprechenden Wörter während des Hörens ohne vorherige Vokabelvorgabe erfordert. Hier schließt sich wiederum eine *movie synopsis* mit integrierter Vokabelarbeit an (WS 6).

Der Film *Bend It Like Beckham* wurde von Kritiken differenziert aufgenommen. Oft wurde dem Film eine gewisse Oberflächlichkeit vorgeworfen, da er viele intra- und interkulturelle Konflikte, aber auch das Thema der Homosexualität zwar spielerisch anspricht und andeutet, dabei jedoch nicht das gesamte Konfliktpotenzial ausleuchtet oder entsprechende ernsthafte Konsequenzen betont.

Vor diesem Hintergrund bietet sich die Arbeit mit einer Filmkritik an, die intertextuell als weitere Textsorte in die Unterrichtsreihe aufgenommen wird (WS 7a/7b). Diese Filmkritik aus *The Observer* (2002) enthält einige anspruchsvolle Vokabeln, die in einer Aufgabenstellung aufgenommen werden, um so der Erweiterung des Wortschatzes der Lernenden zu dienen. Nach nochmaligem Lesen der Filmkritik werden Details aus dem Text entnommen (WS 8). Dies sollte auf das eigene Schreiben einer Filmkritik zu einem selbst gewählten Film hinführen, was durch ein Arbeitsblatt angeleitet wird (WS 9). Die Ankündigung, diese Kritiken etwa auf www.amazon.com zu veröffentlichen, könnte hierbei motivierend sein.

Abschließend bieten die im Extramaterial der DVD enthaltenen Interviews mit den Schauspielern und der Regisseurin den Ansatz für eine Hör- und Diskussionsaufgabe (WS 10a/10b).

Bend It Like Beckham: Worksheet 1

Movie posters

Task 1: Have a look at the two movie posters. From the two examples, can you predict the movie's story?

Task 2: Which of the two posters do you like better? Would you be compelled to see the movie? Why? Why not?

Task 3: How do the posters differ? In how far are they the same?

Poster 1	Poster 2

Task 4: List the features a movie poster traditionally consists of.

1 ______________________________
2 ______________________________
3 ______________________________
4 ______________________________
5 ______________________________

⌛____ minutes

Sequence 1: Role expectations (0:00:00 - 0:23:52)

Mr. Bhamra tells his daughter Jessminder: "You must start behaving like a proper woman." Jules's mother fears that playing football would make her daughter less feminine: "All I'm saying is, there is a reason why Sporty Spice is the only one of them without a fellow."

Jessminder's father and Beckham

Jules's mother and football

Task 1: In the table below list items that apparently define "femininity" for Mr. and Mrs. Bhamra (Punjabi/Sikh) and for Mrs. Paxton (British).

Mr. & Mrs. Bhamra	Mrs. Paxton

Task 2: Which kind of expectations are boys and girls / men and women confronted with in Germany? Discuss.

⧖___ minutes

Sequence 2: Culture clash(es) (0:23:52 – 0:48:47) 

Bend It Like Beckham *touches upon instances of culture clash between the British and the Punjabi community. However, matters turn out to be more complicated as the movie also presents us with other "clashes" as well.*

The younger generation taking over?

Task: Comment on how the discussion below between Jessminder and her parents illustrates the fact that there is more than one "clash" in the movie?

Mr. Bhamra: "When I was a teenager in Nairobi I was the best fastballer. [...] But when I came to this country – nothing. I was not allowed to play in any of the teams and these bloody goras made fun of my turban and sent me off packing. [...] None of our boys are in any of the football leagues; you think they will let our girls?"

Jess: "But that is what's changing now. Look at Nasser Hussein, he is captain of the England cricket team. He is Asian!"

Mrs. Bhamra: "Hussein is a Muslim name. Their families are different."

 ____ minutes

Sequence 3: Racism (0:48:47 - 1:13:10)

The movie shows an instance of racism when Jessminder is sent off the pitch for pushing a player who had called her a "paki".

Racism

Racism is hostile and/or oppressive behavior towards people because they belong to a different culture. The belief that one culture is superior to another may be so deeply embedded in the dominant culture that it is not questioned but taken for granted. Once taken for granted, racism may even be displayed by institutions and their representatives.

Jessminder is sent off the pitch by the referee

Task 1: If you were in Jessminder's shoes, how would this situation make you feel? Tick the adjectives that best describe her reaction/emotions. Defend your choice.

- ☐ angry
- ☐ joyful
- ☐ delighted
- ☐ frustrated
- ☐ frantic
- ☐ annoyed
- ☐ discouraged
- ☐ upset
- ☐ hurt
- ☐ hysterical

Task 2: How does Joe, Jessminder's coach, react? Elaborate.

Notes:____

____

____

____

Bend It Like Beckham: Worksheet 4b

Task 3: Imagine yourself to be in Jessminder's or Joe's shoes. Write a diary entry in which you deal with your feelings in this situation.

Diary entry:____________________________________

⌛ ____ minutes

Sequence 4: A happy ending (1:13:10 – 1:47:32)

When Mr. Bhamra delivers his moving speech at the end of the movie, he conveys its major message.

Mr. Bhamra giving his speech

Task 1: Watch (and listen to) the movie sequence (1:34:25 - 1:35:20) twice and fill in the gaps in the transcript below.

> Mr. Bhamra: "When those bloody English (1) ________ players threw me out of their club like a (2) ________, I never complained. On the contrary, I (3) __________ I would never play again. Who (4) __________? Me. But I don't want Jessie to suffer. I don't want her to make the same mistakes that her father made, of (5) _________________ life, accepting situations. I want her to (6) _________. And I want her to win. [...] I don't think (7) _______________ has the right of stopping her.

Task 2: Considering Mr. Bhamra's words, what may be the major message of the movie?

⌛____ minutes

Bend It Like Beckham: Worksheet 6

Movie synopsis

Task: Fill in the gaps with appropriate words from the vocabulary box.

The movie captures the story of the Punjabi teenage girl, Jesminder "Jess" Bhamra, who lives in a (1) __________ of London not far from Heathrow Airport. Her first-generation Punjabi immigrant parents push her hard to study to get into university and become a lawyer. They also wish to arrange a marriage for her in due course. Jessminder, caught between two worlds – her Punjabi (2) _____________ and British culture –, instead dreams of football. She is inspired by one of England's most famous players, David Beckham, and displays unusual (3) _________ at the game in park matches with the local boys. Spotted by Juliette "Jules", the star player at a local (4) ___________ football club, she decides to join the club.

Jess becomes a (5) ___________ and makes friends with the team's coach, a young former player whose dreams of fame were shattered when he injured his knee. The resulting situation sets up a number of culture (6) _________ ranging from the comical to the serious, as Jessminder is confronted with demands both from within the Asian (7) _______________ and the football club. She therefore has to try to accommodate the (8) __________ __________ of two cultures to her own dreams and desires.

The movie also demonstrates that immigrant families are not unique in their adherence to tradition. Furthermore, a parallel subplot evolves, in which Jules's mother, who has very conventional (9) ______________ of femininity, mistakenly believes that Jules is in a homosexual (10) __________________ with Jessminder.

Instead of following the conventions of the uncompromising father and the understanding mother, the roles are reversed. Jessminder's father has the wisdom to let his daughter fulfill her dreams, while her mother puts down her foot and demands that Jessminder follow Punjabi (11) __________. In the end, both Jess and Jules have solved the conflict with their mothers and leave for the USA, where they have been offered a football (12) ________ ___________.

Vocabulary box

upbringing	community	skill
scholarship	suburb	clashes
women's	key player	views
expectations	traditions	relationship

⌛___ minutes

Movie review

Task 1: Read the movie review below carefully.

The conventional wisdom in the film industry is that sports movies are a poor investment because they don't **attract** women. Not even when they're about women. [...] Robert Towne's film about female athletes, *Personal Best*, was a major disaster. [...] This brings us to Gurinder Chadha's *Bend It Like Beckham*, the **heroine** of which is a soccer-mad Indian girl from west London and (unless there's some **innuendo** that eludes me) refers to David Beckham's brilliance at getting a ball into the net around a wall of defenders. Chadha, whose **previous** films are *Bhaji on the Beach* and *What's Cooking?*, makes feel-good comedies of ethnic manners. Difficult questions of race relations and the accommodation of tradition to social change are swept under the carpets on which the casts dance. While recognisably her work, *Bend It Like Beckham* is **coarser** and more ambitious than the earlier films. Her delightful protagonist, Jess Bhamra, is a bright 18-year-old schoolgirl, daughter of Sikhs from East Africa. Dad works at Heathrow and they live comfortably in a semi-detached under the flight path in Hounslow, trying to hold on to old ways. The anglicised Jess fantasises about playing alongside Beckham for Manchester United and having her performance **appraised** on TV by Gary Lineker, Alan Hansen and John Barnes. Of course her parents think soccer is dangerously unfeminine and when, through a lower-middle-class English **chum**, Jules, she gets a trial with the all-girl Hounslow Harriers she has to keep it a secret.

From this point on every **cliché** of the sports drama and of the family comedy flow freely [...]. Jess would have impressed Houdini with her **skill** in fooling her **gullible** parents so she can get out of the house to play with her team. When depressed she loses her form, but regains it the moment results matter. Every game ends with a cliffhanging shot at goal. Naturally the all-important match that will be watched by a scout for an American university coincides with her sister's wedding. On at least four occasions Jess is seen in an innocent **embrace** which the observer misinterprets (in one case she's taken to be a lesbian). In the final scenes liberal ecumenicism runs riot as everyone comes to **appreciate** everyone else's religion and tastes. Jess abandons the prospect of a legal career in Britain and **heads off** with a football scholarship to California, where Chadha herself now lives.

There are plenty of **chuckles** and smart lines in this relentlessly cheerful movie. One thinks especially of a remark by the primly conventional mother of Jess's best friend, deploring her passion for soccer: "There's a reason why Sporty Spice is the only one without a fellow." The games themselves are impressively edited. But the script by Chadha and her American husband, Paul Mayeda Berges (who also worked as second unit director), takes every easy way out and never recognises the possibility of real pain, the way the tougher, far funnier *East Is East* does.

(adapted from a review by Philip French, *The Observer*, April 14, 2002)

Bend It Like Beckham: Worksheet 7b

Task 2: Match the words from the text (left column) with their synonyms in the right column. If necessary, use a monolingual dictionary and/or thesaurus.

(1) attract	________________	hug
(2) heroine	________________	more critical
(3) innuendo	________________	female lead
(4) previous	________________	truism
(5) coarser	________________	earlier
(6) appraised	________________	talent
(7) chum	________________	honored
(8) skill	________________	friend
(9) gullible	________________	undertone
(10) embrace	________________	leaves
(11) appreciate	________________	understand
(12) cliché	________________	catch the attention of
(13) heads off	________________	giggles
(14) chuckles	________________	naïve

Task 3: Choose three words from the right-hand column and write 3 sentences of your own in which you use these words.

(1)____

____

____

(2)____

____

____

(3)____

____

____

⌛____ minutes

Structure of reviews

Task: Re-read the movie review and fill in the worksheet below.

	Review "Bend It Like Beckham"
(1) Source/reviewer	
(2) Positive features of the movie discussed	
(3) Features criticized by the reviewer	
(4) Summary of the reviewer's opinion	
(5) Find keywords to summarize the content of each of the three paragraphs	(1) (2) (3)

⌛____ minutes

Writing a review

Task: Write your own movie review about a movie you have recently seen. Include your impressions, critical reflections, and your opinion. Follow the structure discussed in class and summarized in the outline below.

Introduction

You can begin with information about the film (e.g. awards, reviews) and/or the director (e.g. former films, autobiographical data). Quotes and/or anecdotes may catch the reader's attention. Your introduction should also include a brief summary of the movie.

Opinion (Main part)

State your opinion of the film and give reasons for it. What are its strengths and weaknesses? Support your opinion with specific scenes, the actors' performances, etc. Describe the director's intention. What is special about the movie, its theme, and its actors?

Recommendation (Conclusion)

Can you recommend the film? Take care that your final judgement is logically developed from what you have written before.

⌛____ minutes

Interviews

Task 1: Listen to the interviews with the actors and the director of the movie. Who said what? Match two sentences with each picture.

Parminder Nagra

Keira Knightley

Anupam Kher

Juliet Stevenson

(g) "It's not poking fun at people at their expense."

(h) "I think it's just all about growing up."

(i) "What so many girls have to do is bend the rules to get what they want."

Archie Panjabi

(j) "She is completely obsessed with her one beloved daughter."

(k) "Our girls want to aim for the top, go out, and achieve it."

Gurinder Chadha

(l) "It's quite universal in that respect."

Task 2: Discuss and comment on the meaning and context of these utterances.

Movie posters (worksheet 1, p. 47)

Poster 1 (British, 2002)	Poster 2 (American, 2003)
reviews from British newspapers	reviews from American newspapers
references to Bridget Jones's Diary and David Beckham	no reference to other movies, star rating
picture shows both Jessminder and Jules	picture shows only parts of Jessminder's head with a football on top
the colors chosen are moderate (green and white)	the colors (pink and blue) create a vivid contrast
the audience is invited to come to the cinema (British term)	the poster mentions the (movie) theater (American term)

Features of a movie poster

1 title of the movie
2 stars in the movie
3 director of the movie
4 strap line as advertisement for the movie
5 picture to draw attention to the movie

Sequence 1: Role expectations (worksheet 2, p. 48)

Girls are confronted with different demands from their parents: Jessminder is supposed to be successful at school and to become a solicitor. She is not meant to go out with boys unless a marriage comes out of that relationship as is the case with Pinkie, her older sister. Jessminder is supposed to wear traditional clothes and help her mother at home. Jules is pressured by her mother to become more feminine. She apparently does not like the way Jules dresses – more like a boy than a girl, in her opinion. A push-up bra is supposed to enhance her female appeal. To Jules's mother, playing football is a distinctly unfeminine activity. It makes her daughter less feminine and even fuels her fears of Jules being in a homosexual relationship.

Sequence 2: Culture clash(es) (worksheet 3, p. 49)

The culture clash in the movie is not presented as one entirely caused by differences between the Punjabi/Sikh and the British community. Consider, for example, the scene in the changing room. Jessminder tells the other players that she could never marry a White, Black, or Muslim boy. An Indian boy would be her only choice. When the parents of Pinkie's boyfriend visit the Bhamras, they call off the marriage because Jessminder has brought shame onto the family. Like the dialogue on the worksheet, these scenes reinforce the director's attempt to show that intracultural and generational conflicts in the Punjabi/Sikh community cause conflicts as well.

Sequence 3: Racism (worksheets 4a/4b, p. 50-51)

Jess is called a "paki" by one of the players of the other team. This term is a derogatory expression for a Pakistani. Here, prejudices against the Pakistani community are projected onto Jessminder, who is not even Pakistani but a Sikh. This shows the superficial nature of stereotypes. What is more, even the referee seems to play an active part in this display of racism. He sends Jessminder off the pitch for pushing another player although Jessminder had been fouled and called a "paki" first. The referee does not punish this behavior. This is evidence to the effect that racist attitudes may even be displayed by objective judges.

Bend It Like Beckham: Answer key

Sequence 4: A happy ending (worksheet 5, p. 52)

In a look back onto his own life, Jessminder's father realizes the mistakes he has made. He understands that withdrawing from British culture or giving up the fight against prejudices is not a valid solution. The message Jessminder's father conveys in this scene is that of individual freedom and the right to try to accomplish one's wishes and goals against all odds.

(1) cricket (2) dog (3) vowed (4) suffered (5) accepting (6) fight (7) anyone

Movie synopsis (worksheet 6, p. 53)

(1) suburb (2) upbringing (3) skill (4) women's (5) key player (6) clashes (7) community (8) expectations (9) views (10) relationship (11) traditions (12) scholarship

Movie review (worksheets 7a/7b, p. 54-55)

(1) attract – to catch the attention of
(2) heroine – female lead
(3) innuendo – undertone
(4) previous – earlier
(5) coarser – more critical
(6) appraised – honored
(7) chum – friend
(8) cliché – truism
(9) skill – talent
(10) gullible – naive
(11) embrace – to hug
(12) appreciate – to understand
(13) heads off – to leave
(14) chuckles – giggles

Structure of reviews (worksheet 8, p. 56)

	Review "Bend It Like Beckham"
(1) Source/reviewer	Philip French (The Observer)
(2) Positive features of the movie discussed	feel-good comedies of ethnic manners, coarser, more ambitious than earlier movies
(3) Features criticized by the reviewer	questions of race relations are swept under the carpet, clichés, conventional
(4) Summary of the reviewer's opinion	The movie could have been more critical. Chadha takes the easy way out.
(5) Find keywords to summarize the content of each of the three paragraphs	(1) introduction, (2) opinion (main part), (3) recommendation (conclusion)

Interviews (worksheets 10a/10b, p. 58-59)

Parminder Nagra: b, d
Keira Knightley: a, f
Anupam Kher: c, e
Juliet Stevenson: g, j
Archie Panjabi: h, l
Gurinder Chadha: i, k

Mise en scène:

Storyboard: a series of drawings used to illustrate the sequence of a shot
Screenplay (script): a description of the action and dialogue of a movie
Plot: the events presented in a movie, including causal relations, chronological order, duration, frequency, etc.
Flashback: a shot or a sequence of shots that moves back in time, then returns to the present
Flashforward: a shot or a sequence of shots in which the plot moves forward to the future and then returns
Setting: the place, time period and circumstances of the story line
Location: the place where the filming takes place (either on location or on the set)
Cast(ing): the group of actors who perform in a movie/process of selecting actors
Lead/leading role: the most important character in a movie
Supporting role: a less important role to the leading actor or actress
Minor Role: a small part in a movie, a walk-on part (often not involving speaking)

Cinematography:

Camera Distance: the distance between camera and filmed object/subject and/or setting
Close-up (CU): a shot framing the head from the neck up
Medium close-up (MCU): usually a human figure filmed from the chest up
Extreme close-up (ECU): the screen is filled by a part of someone's face
Medium shot (MS): a framing usually showing a human figure from the waist up
Medium long shot (MLS): a framing showing a human figure from the knees up
Long shot (LS): a framing showing a human figure from above the head to below the feet
Extreme long shot (ELS): a distant shot providing a panoramic view of an exterior location
Establishing shot: framed from a distance it shows the setting in relation to important figures and objects

Camera Perspective:

High-angle shot (bird's-eye view): a shot looking down on the action
Low-Angle shot: a shot looking up at the action
Eye-level shot: a shot implying the normal way of seeing
Dutch angle (canted angle): a shot in which the camera is tipped sideways
Point of view shot (POV): a shot representing what a character sees before/after a shot of the character looking
Over-the-shoulder shot (OTS): a shot framed over the shoulder of a character looking at another character
Wide (angle) shot (WS): a shot taking in much or all of the action

Glossar

CAMERA MOVEMENT:

ZOOM: creates the impression of the camera moving closer to the photographed object/subject without camera movement (the focal length of the zoom lens is altered)

PAN: from panorama or panoramic, the camera, positioned on a stationary tripod, moves on a vertical line from left to right (or vice versa) scanning the space horizontally

TILT: the camera, positioned on a stationary support, swivels upward or downward scanning the space vertically

TRACKING SHOT: a shot taken with a camera positioned on a dolly or a moving vehicle

CRANE SHOT: a shot from a great height photographed by a camera mounted on a crane

HAND-HELD CAMERA: the camera is held by an operator without the help of a fixed mounting causing irregular movement often signifying point of view

FREEZE FRAME: a freeze shot of a particular frame to create the illusion of a still photograph

LIGHTING:

BACKLIGHTING: lighting cast on the figures from behind to create a thin outline of light on the figures' edges thus creating a mystical and tense atmosphere

FRONTAL LIGHTING: lighting cast on the figures from a source positioned near the camera

SIDE LIGHTING: lighting coming from a source positioned on one side of a person, usually to create tension or to fill in areas left shadowed by light from another source

TOP LIGHTING: lighting coming from above a person in order to stress the upper areas of a figure or to cast a figure in an unfavorable light making the character look exhausted

UNDERLIGHTING: lighting from a source below the figures in the scene, creating shadows and thus causing the figure to appear dangerous and/or threatening

LOW-KEY LIGHTING: poor intensity of light creating shadowy areas and a strong contrast between light and dark areas of the shot

HIGH-KEY LIGHTING: lighting creating relatively little contrast between the light and dark areas of the shot

HARD LIGHTING: an intensity of lighting that creates sharp edges

SOFT LIGHTING: less intense and bright light avoiding sharp edges, instead creating a gradual transition from light to shadow

Editing:

Shot/reverse shot: alternating shots of two characters in a dialogue scene (often over-the-shoulder framing)

Reaction shot: a shot in which we see a character's reaction to something

Parallel editing (cross-cutting): editing that alternates between two or more different shots, linking or contrasting the shots which usually develop simultaneously

Split screen: two shots developing simultaneously on a screen usually split into two halves

Cut: a clean break and instantaneous jump from one framing to another

Jump cut: a shot comparable to an ellipsis interrupting a shot in order to condense it

Match cut: two shots are linked visually, aurally, or metaphorically

Fast-cutting: a fast-paced succession of shots of comparably brief duration in order to create an atmosphere of energy, emergency, urgency, etc.

Slow-cutting: a slow-paced succession of shots of comparably long duration to create an atmosphere of peace, tranquility, and serenity

Slow motion: a way of filming in which the action is made to appear slower than normal

Fade out/in: a take in which the image of a shot gradually fades into black and a consecutive image gradually appears from out of the black screen

Sound:

Sound effects: audio components usually created by Foley artists and integrated into the movie during post-production

Soundtrack: the collection of the songs chosen for the movie to support the atmosphere of specific scenes, to enhance emotions, or even to structure the movie

Dub: a technique by which a movie is provided mainly with monologues, dialogues, and voice-overs (sometimes with a soundtrack) in a different language

Voice-over: the voice of an unseen commentator or narrator heard during a movie